教育部学校规划建设发展中心、重庆第二师范学院儿童研究院重点项目“核心素养背景下小学英语融思促学活动设计与研究”（批准号：CRIKT202006）研究成果

核心素养背景下小学英语融思促学活动设计研究

HEXIN SUYANG BEIJINGXIA XIAOXUE YINGYU RONGSI CUXUE HUODONG SHEJI YANJIU

周利君　雷涵彧　汪兴楣　编著

重庆大学出版社

图书在版编目（CIP）数据

核心素养背景下小学英语融思促学活动设计研究 / 周利君，雷涵彧，汪兴楣编著. --重庆：重庆大学出版社，2021.7

ISBN 978-7-5689-2688-1

Ⅰ. ①核… Ⅱ. ①周… ②雷… ③汪… Ⅲ. ①英语课—教学设计—小学 Ⅳ. ① G623.312

中国版本图书馆CIP数据核字（2021）第085005号

核心素养背景下小学英语融思促学活动设计研究

周利君 雷涵彧 汪兴楣 编著

责任编辑：陈 亮 版式设计：周永梅 陈 亮

责任校对：陈 力 责任印制：赵 晟

*

重庆大学出版社出版发行

出版人：饶帮华

社址：重庆市沙坪坝区大学城西路21号

邮编：401331

电话：（023）88617190 88617185（中小学）

传真：（023）88617186 88617166

网址：http://www.cqup.com.cn

邮箱：fxk@cqup.com.cn（营销中心）

全国新华书店经销

重庆俊蒲印务有限公司印刷

*

开本：787mm × 1092mm 1/16 印张：10.5 字数：254千

2021年7月第1版 2021年7月第1次印刷

ISBN 978-7-5689-2688-1 定价：49.00元

序（一）

记得2011年，我在北京给小学教师做讲座的时候提到如何通过英语教学培养学生的思维能力，很多教师还不是很理解。当时主流的观点是：外语教学首先要培养学生的语言能力，要积累一定的语言技能、词汇、语法、句型等，然后才能谈别的方面。如果学生没有这些语言的基础，就无法培养思维能力。

实际上，学生从学习语言的第一天开始，就涉及思维能力的培养。我访问过好几所美国的小学，儿童在学前就已经开始进行思维能力的培养，比如区分“事实与观点（facts or opinions）”。几乎每所学校，都把要培养的几种思维能力，贴在教室墙上，这给我留下了深刻的印象。

我想，初学英语的学生，虽然开始接触的语言很少，但是完全可以培养思维能力。举个例子：苹果有营养是“事实”，某种苹果最好吃是“观点”。只是我们的教师需要知道，应该培养哪些方面的思维能力，比如说：原因和结果、分类、推断、归纳等；更为重要的是：教师们还需要知道，如何培养这些思维能力，什么任务活动有助于培养这些思维能力，可以借助什么工具等。

最近几年，随着国家课程标准的修订，关于培养学生核心素养的要求已成为教师们讨论的热点话题，特别是品格培养和思维培养这两个方面。教师们感到，基础教育的目标应该是人的全面发展，必须培养学生的思维能力和品格。但是，究竟如何做，对思维的分类、内涵、范畴等，现在还缺乏明确的定义，更缺乏非常清晰的指导。到底培养学生哪些方面的思维能力，通过什么样的活动能培养这些思维能力，教师们缺乏现成的、方便实用的资料。我很高兴看到，重庆第二师范学院周利君老师带领的团队设计出这样一套适合小学高段学生和教师使用的小学英语融思促学活动资源。这真是及时雨!

这套活动资源可用于学生学习、亲子学习，也可用作教师教学的补充资源或提高教师专业知识与能力的学习材料。所以在这里，一方面，我要对周老师及其团队表示衷心的祝贺；另一方面，也希望有更多的中小学英语教师能积极应用这套活动资源，将发展学生的思维能力、良好品格和行为习惯与培养英语运用能力结合起来。我也希望有更多的教师，能受到这套活动资源的启发，在自己的学校开展各种创造性的活动，共同铺建英语教育的新路。

龚亚夫

2020年7月4日

序（二）

Manual of Integrating Teaching Thinking to Primary English Classes in the Context of Key Competencies is published at a time when there are global recognitions of the need and importance of thinking skills into the English education curricula. In 2017, nurturing students' thinking skills was explicitly stated in English education curriculum for basic education. Despite an overall positive response to the new learning objectives, how to integrate teaching thinking into language classrooms has been in discussion by both practitioners and researchers. This manual has provided teachers some practical answers and useful examples on "what" and "how".

The knowledge of thinking skills was identified as a main factor of integrating them into language teaching. Working with language teachers both in the UK and in China and postgraduates attending my module of "Thinking Skills in English Language Teaching" has consistently confirmed that to integrate thinking skills into language classrooms is more than adding a few tasks into a lesson plan. Teachers need to understand what thinking skills activities look like so that they can design activities that require higher order thinking. This manual provides a useful tool for teachers to assess the expected level of cognitive requirement of activities they have designed or in a textbook based on revised Bloom's taxonomy.

Increasing research shows positive effect of teaching thinking on language learning, though concerns were repeatedly reported on appropriateness of introducing thinking skills to primary school students due to their limited language ability. As an outcome of collaborations between researchers and school teachers, this manual presents workable examples of what can be done with primary school students. Content in each unit is carefully planned. Activities are organised coherently and progressively in order to prepare students for thinking skills embedded activities. Relevant learning contexts and language support are also considered and provided to enable students to carry out activities, including language to express thinking.

Another revealing feature of this manual lies in the design of the activities. They reflect good practice in English language teaching and those promoted in recent English language reforms. Last two decades has witnessed a number of new reforms, including promoting student-centred teaching approach, emphasising on developing students' learning strategies and problem-solving abilities, and ability to use English for communication. Teaching of vocabulary and grammar rules in this manual concurs with learning through using language for doing. Reversing the usual present practice and product teaching sequence, students are encouraged to work out meaning or rules themselves through comparison or contrast or problem-solving activities. Comparison and contrast are the basics of thinking skills.

Various interesting and current visual images suitable for young learners are used to motivate and encourage students to think in English. A number of graphs or organisers are available to nurture students' thinking and help them carry out problem-solving and decision-making tasks.

Developing thinking skills embedded language teaching materials requires time and effort. This manual has done the groundwork and provided a lot of creative ideas and practical suggestions and examples, in particular closely linked to topics in the teaching textbook used by majority of primary teachers. These ideas can be adapted to other contexts or levels. Congratulations to all the teachers, students and university lecturers who participated in producing this wonderful manual. Well done! I sincerely hope that more teachers will join in the explorations of ways to integrate teaching thinking in language classrooms. I am looking forward to more examples and practice.

Mei Lin

Senior Lecturer

School of Education, Communication and Language Sciences

Newcastle University, UK

前 言

语言是思维的外壳，思维是语言的内在。核心素养背景下，学习者语言能力与思维能力同步发展成为广大一线教师开展英语教学改革与科学研究的重要课题之一。

布鲁姆等1956年提出的教育目标分类体系被国际教育界广泛采用。随着分类体系研究的发展，安德森等汇集认知心理学、课程研究、教育研究和语言测试等方面的研究成果，发布了更符合21世纪教育教学改革发展的教育目标分类体系修订版，主要包括认知过程和知识两个维度。其中，认知过程维度包括六大类别，每一类别下面又包含若干子类别的思维技能，形成由易到难、由简单到复杂的目标层次结构。相对于思维能力，思维技能理解难度系数低，以特定的思维理论框架作为英语教学的依托、涵盖不同层级思维技能的训练，在教学中具有更强的实操性。融入式思维教学将思维训练贯穿于学科日常教学中，与学科教学相辅相成。

2015年以来，重庆第二师范学院外国语言文学学院通过巴渝海外引智计划引进英国纽卡斯尔大学林梅博士和汉纳肯博士，联合开展“外语教育融思促学教研团队”（以下简称“团队”）建设，对合作基地小学优秀师资和院内英语师范专业优秀学子进行培养。在这个过程中，团队多次深入一线小学英语课堂教学观摩，发现小学英语教学多重语言知识技能，轻思维训练，其主要原因在于思维理论框架复杂且较抽象，缺乏教材配套思维训练资源。自

2018年开始，团队积极致力于外语教育融思促学资源开发。2018年年底，团队选送第一批完成的融思促学活动参加国家未来学校博览会，受到来自市内外参会一线教师的肯定与欢迎。团队大受鼓舞，结合在合作基地学校开展的融思促学实验研究开发了小学英语融思促学活动，供小学高段学生和教师使用。

本套活动资源与以人教版为代表的现行小学英语教材（六年级）单元话题配套，从课标中各话题下语言知识和语言技能学习要求出发，提供语言知识学习和语言技能训练的活动。单元编写体例采用“top-down”的语言学习理念，从语言技能到语言知识，整体特点鲜明，具体如下：

思维技能融入的显性化。显性化途径多元，一是在活动步骤中凸显思维技能的动词表达并不断重复，有助于师生理解和记忆。二是在活动过程说明之后采用思维试纸，将活动步骤与对应的思维层级相匹配，有利于教师明确所设计活动的认知复杂度，并检查单元活动设计的思维层级的多样性。三是在活动步骤旁运用提示贴纸，凸显思维工具和策略的使用说明，促使教师有意识地引导学生借助思维工具和策略强化思维训练。

思维技能融入的具体化。针对一线教师在英语教学中融入思维训练太过抽象，不知道如何在课堂中实现这一问题，活动设计从一线教师角度，模拟教案形式，对教学目标设定和教学活动步骤、教学建议等进行了具体说明，帮助教师快速进入融入式教学实践。部分活动步骤说明还提供了多种方案和实施建议，给予教师空间根据自身课堂情况进行筛选和调整。

思维技能融入的全面性。思维训练方面，依据修订版的布鲁姆教育目标分类框架的认知维度，覆盖低阶思维技能和高阶思维技能。结合各单元主题情境，教学活动设计兼顾基础思维技能活动和复杂思维过程任务，关注单个技能和复杂思维的同步训练。语言教学方面，每个单元采用从整体到局部的教学思路，从听、说、读、写等语言技能入手，落实到词汇、语法等语言知识的学习，满足不同的语言教学需求。

本套活动资源是教育部学校规划建设发展中心、重庆第二师范学院儿童研究院重点项目“核心素养背景下小学英语融思促学活动设计与研究”（批准号：CRIKT202006）的成果，由课题负责人周利君组织设计、主持编写、审校定稿。其中6A部分由雷涵彧、周利君编写完成，6B部分由汪兴楣、周利君编写完成。贺倩彧、孙亮参与统稿，部分活动由单芳、邬若环在合作基地小学进行了课堂实践后提出修订建议。本套活动资源编写过程中，得到了重庆第二师范学院外国语言文学学院领导和同事、巴渝海外引智专家、基地学校领导和同行的大力支持，在此表示衷心感谢。

由于课题组成员水平有限，难免有错漏之处，敬请各位专家和同行批评指正。

周利君

2021年2月

Contents

目 录

6A

Unit 1 How Can I Get There? ······ 2

Unit 2 Ways to Go to School ······ 17

Unit 3 My Weekend Plan ······ 32

Unit 4 I Have a Pen Pal ······ 45

Unit 5 What Does He Do? ······ 58

Unit 6 How Do You Feel? ······ 72

6B

Unit 1 How Tall Are You? ······ 88

Unit 2 Last Weekend ······ 106

Unit 3 Where Did You Go? ······ 125

Unit 4 Then and Now ······ 141

6A

Unit 1 How Can I Get There?

单元导览

单元话题: 描述路线/使用地图

素材来源: PEP 6A Unit 1 How Can I Get There?

教学目标:

By the end of the lessons, students will be able to

语言目标:

1. **understand** conversations in the textbook, **describe** places they know in daily life (e.g. bookstore, cinema, science museum, post office, hospital, etc.) and what they can do in these places;

2. **give** guidance to others about how to get to a place and ask for directions (How can I get…?/ It's next to/near/behind…; Go straight; Turn left/right at…);

3. **explain** the reasons why they like going to a specific place and express corresponding feelings;

4. **comprehend** the meaning of the story, **analyze** the main content and structure, and **apply** the knowledge and language in the story to writing about their own ideas in another situation.

非语言目标:

1. **associate** geographic knowledge and life experience about directions when giving guidance;

2. work in groups and collaborate with others to finish tasks related to their daily life about places and directions;

3. strengthen their higher order thinking skills: **analyzing** and **creating**;

4. **design** objects with creative thinking and **judge** with critical thinking.

融思设计

Part One Listening and Speaking

教学素材: Part A & B Let's Talk

教学步骤:

Step 1 Listening Comprehension

1. Listen and **choose** the right answers.

   Part A:

   Where is Wu Yifan?

   A. In the museum shop. B. In the science museum. C. In the post office.

   Part B:

   Where are Mike and Wu Yifan now?

   A. In the bookstore. B. In the cinema. C. In the restaurant.

2. Listen and **match** the items with the related places.

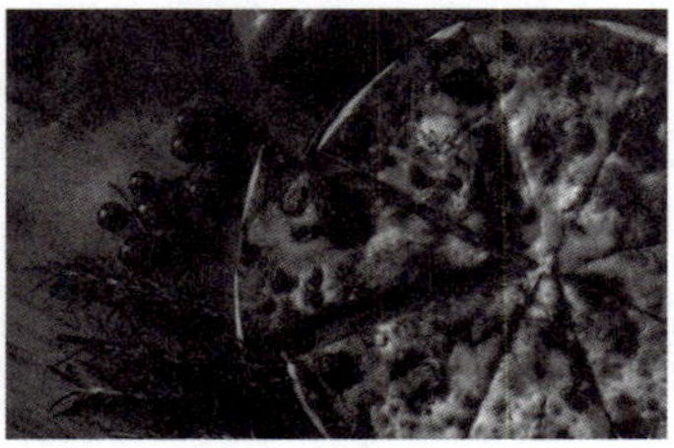

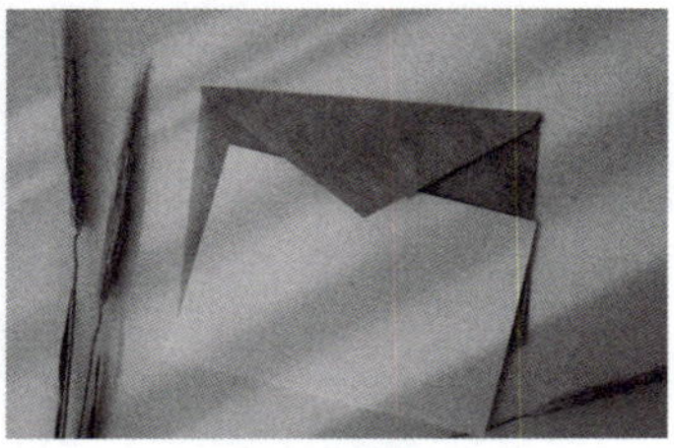

3. **Think about** the reasons why Wu Yifan wants to go to these places, and write down reasons below.

(1) Wu Yifan wants to go to ________ because he can ________ there.
(2) Wu Yifan wants to go to ________ because he can ________ there.

Step 2 Preparation before Speaking

1. **Write down** what you can do in the following places. You can **list** many things and you can also **add** more places.

Bookstore	Cinema	Science Museum	Post Office	Hospital	________	________
read a book	eat popcorn	play with robots	buy stamps	see a dentist	________	________
________	________	________	________	________	________	________

2. If you can go to one place above after school, which place do you want to go to, and what is your reason? You can **use** one sentence pattern below and fill in the blanks.

I like to go to ________ because ________________.
I want to go to ________, so I can ________________.
I want to go to ________ and I don't want to go to ________, because ____________.

Step 3 Speaking and Sharing

1. Work with your partner and recognize the places. You can also **put** 2 places you add from Step 2 in the map.

2. Tell your partner what you want to do, and **ask** he/she where you can go to meet your need.

You	Your Partner
I want to ______________.	You can go to __________
Where can I go?	________________________.

3. Decide a starting point on the map, and **ask** your partner how you can go to the place you want.

Language Kit

— Where is the ___________?

— It's ___________.

— How can I get there?

— Go _______ and turn _________ at the _________.

4. **Write down** your conversation.

A: ________________________________

B: ________________________________

A: ________________________________

B: ________________________________

A: ________________________________

B: ________________________________

教学时长: 1.5 hrs

教学建议:

1. 听力理解环节。

教师可把"Part A"和"Part B"两篇对话结合起来教学。教师播放一遍对话音频，学生完成练习。教师根据学生完成情况可再播放一遍，并订正答案。

2. 表达准备环节。

教师可安排学生在学完两篇对话后完成。

3. 表达与分享环节。

（1）教师检查学生课前完成口语准备的情况，解释任务的逻辑：在不同的地方可以做不同的事情，想去某个地点和在这个地点想做或可以做的事情密切相关。

（2）学生和同伴两人一组，将"Step 2"的表格中提到的地点填到地图中的空白处，学生可以根据个人喜好将地点任意放置。

（3）学生告诉同伴自己想要做的事情，请同伴建议可以去哪个地方做这件事。两人小组可使用提供的句型问答，教师也可以鼓励学生思考是不是只有这个地方能做这件事，有没有其他可能性。

(4) 学生和同伴一起在地图上确定一个起点，根据之前问答中同伴建议去的地点，询问同伴如何到该地点，可参考 “Language Kit” 中给出的句型进行对话。

(5) 两人小组完善对话，并将对话写下来。

思维试纸：

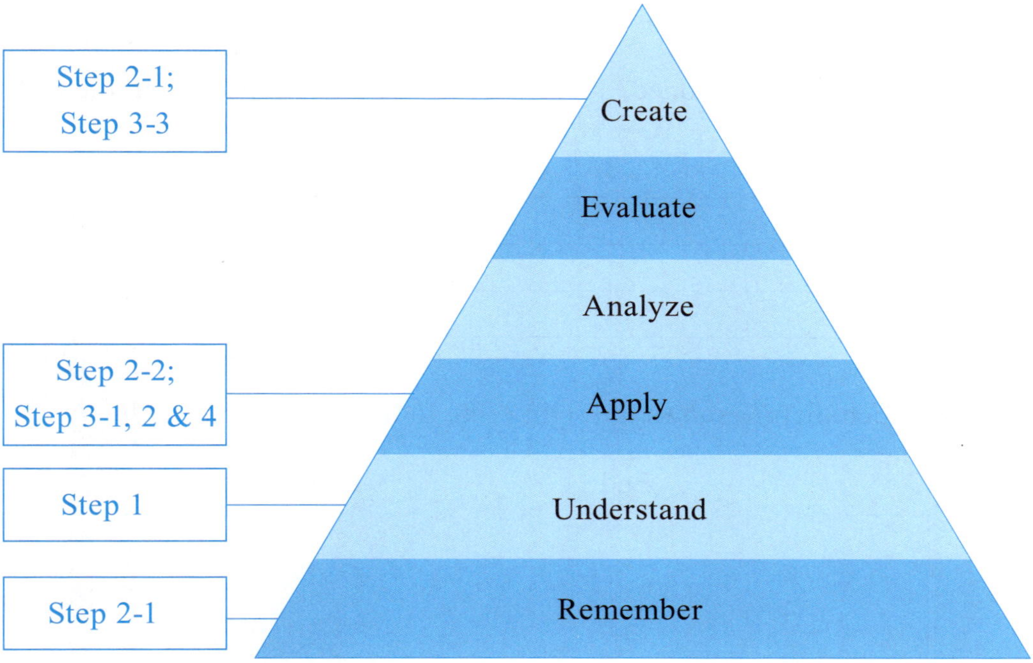

备注：“思维试纸” 将各教学活动中加粗的动词（思维技能）与思维层级匹配，使教学过程中的思维技能训练显性化。6A余下各单元的 “思维试纸” 不再一一备注。

Part Two　Reading and Writing

教学素材：Part B　Read and Write

教学步骤：

Step 1　Preparation before Reading

Read the title “Robin Has GPS!” and **predict** what you will know after reading. You can write down your ideas below.

(1) I will know what GPS can do.

(2) ______________________________

(3) ______________________________

Step 2　Reading Comprehension

1. What places are mentioned? Please **list** all the places you find in the text.

____

____

____

____

2. **Tick** which picture shows the right route to the destination.

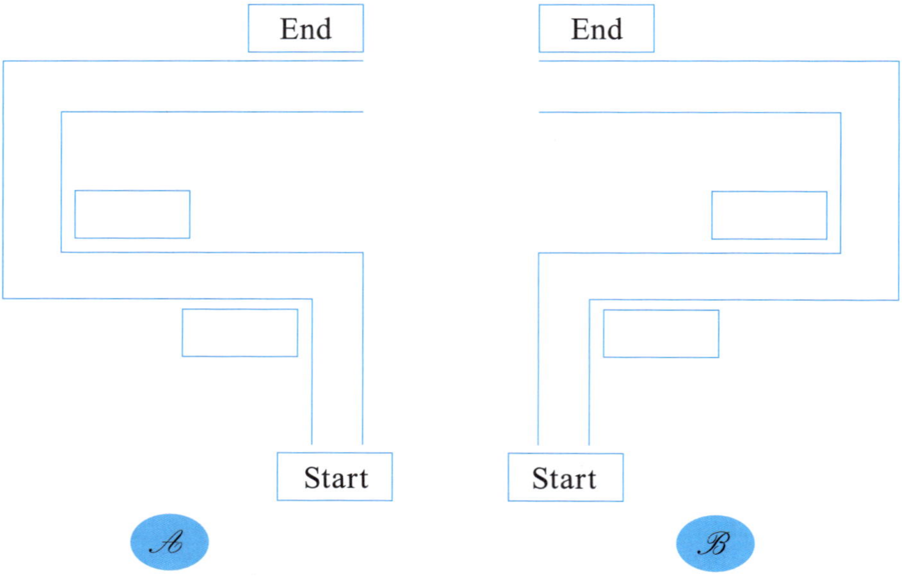

3. What do they want to do to use GPS to find the way? Please read and **choose**.

A. Buy some books.

B. Visit Wu Yifan's grandpa.

C. Eat delicious food.

Step 3 Preparation before Writing

1. This is a brief map of your campus. **Think about** what buildings are on campus and write down names of the buildings in the blank boxes. You should write down at least 5 names.

2. **Think about** what you can do in the places you write in the map, and finish the following chart.

Buildings on Campus		Things You Can Do
library	→	borrow/read books

Step 4 Writing and Sharing

Work with your partner, ask where he/she wants to go on campus, **draw** the route on the map and **complete** the following writing task.

________ wants to go to __________ on campus, because he/she can ________ there. He/She should turn __________, and then _____________.
____
____
______________. Finally, he/she can arrive at the place.

教学时长: 1 hr

教学建议:

1. 读前准备环节。

教师让学生根据文章标题预测文章可能讲述的内容，训练学生预测文本的能力。

2. 阅读理解环节。

学生读完短文后，教师引导学生根据对文章的理解完成相关练习，检验学生对文章大意和部分细节的理解。

3. 写作准备环节。

（1）学生在给出的空白地图上，结合所学内容和个人喜好，填入和校园相关的建筑名称。

（2）根据所填内容，学生思考在不同的地点，可以做哪些事情，为写作环节做准备。

4. 写作与分享环节。

学生和同伴合作完成任务：根据所绘地图，互相询问想去的地点，在地图上画出相应路线，并根据写作提示完成写作练习。

思维试纸:

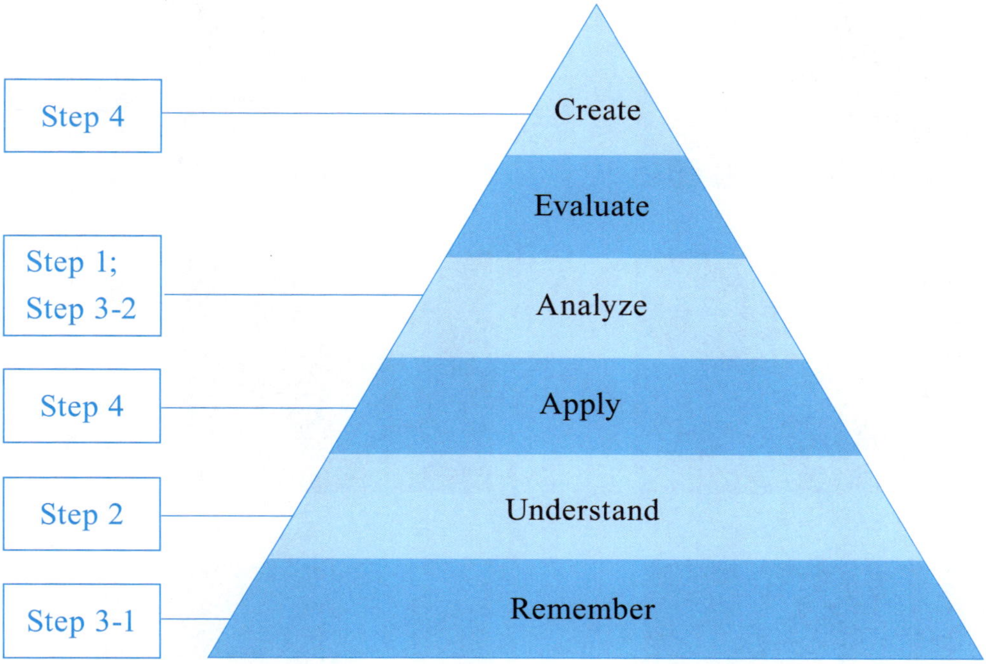

Part Three Vocabulary

教学素材: bookstore, post office, cinema, science museum, post office, GPS, map, compass

教学步骤:

Step 1 Matching and Writing

Match the following items with the places where you can find them, and write down the name of the places.

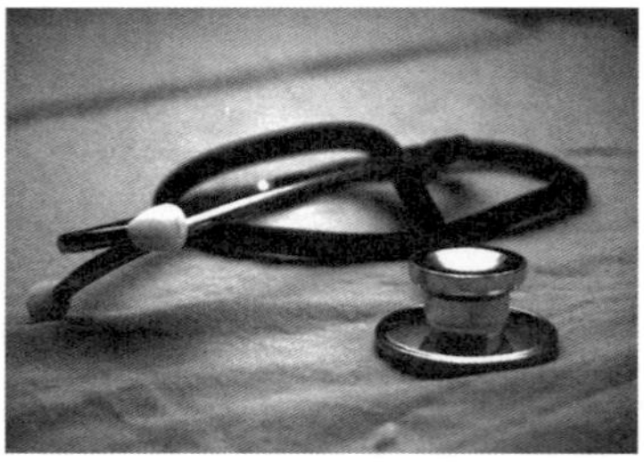

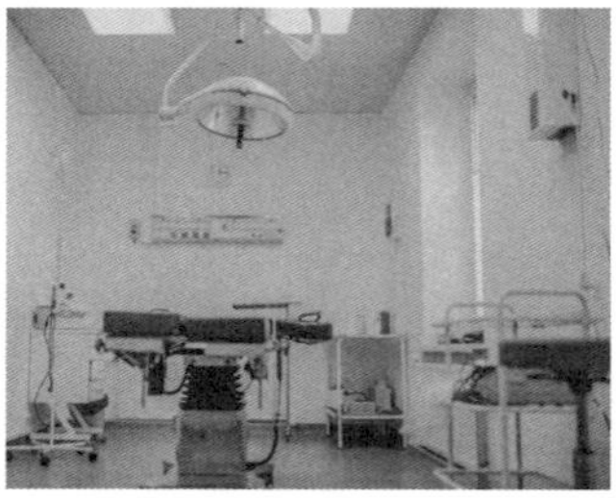

POST OFFICE

Step 2 Blank-filling

Choose one word below and fill in the blanks to **complete** each sentence in a logical way. You can use each word only once.

map compass star GPS

(1) The __________ helps us quickly identify the north, south, west and east.

(2) The __________ helps us know main features of a place, such as its roads and rivers.

(3) The __________ helps us find the position of a person or thing accurately.

(4) The __________ helps us find the north especially in a clear summer night.

教学时长: 15 mins

教学建议:

1. 词汇部分主要用于练习，旨在巩固词汇和语法知识。

2. 学生自行在课前或课后完成，教师批改。

3. 课堂上，教师带领学生总结存在的问题和解决办法，注重巩固学生对本单元重点单词词性、词义的理解。

4. "Step 2" 的参考答案依次为: compass, map, GPS, star。如果单看其中一道题，答案并不是唯一的，如第1题的答案还可以是"star"或"GPS"，但根据题目要求，一个单词只能使用一次，且让每句话都符合逻辑，因此，教师须引导学生注意题目要求，更加全面地思考问题。

思维试纸：

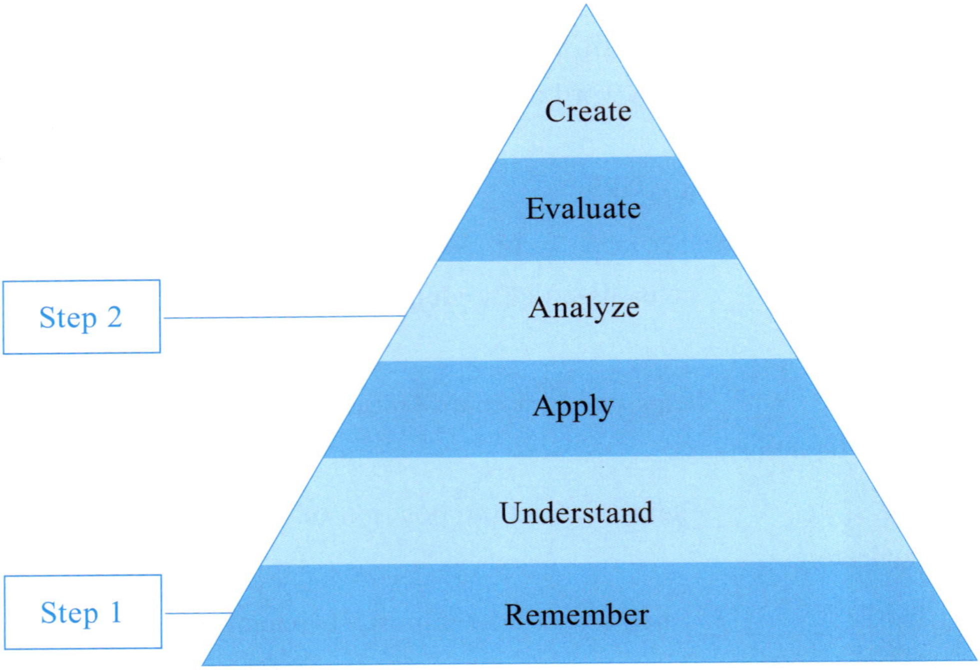

Part Four　Grammar

教学素材：Where is the…?
How can I get the...?
It's near/next to/behind the…
It's over…
Turn left/right at the…
Go straight…

教学步骤：

Step 1　Self-checking

Look at the map and **fill in** the blanks based on the clues given in the conversation.

— Where is the hospital?
— It's ________ the ________.
— How can I get there?
— First, ________. Second, ________. Then, ________.

Step 2 Further Practicing

Look at the map again and complete the sentences below. You need to **infer** the starting point this time.

— ________ is the ________?
— It's next to the science museum.
— ________ can I get there?
— Go straight and turn right at the cinema.

Q: Where is the starting point?
A: It's __________.

Then, you can choose another starting point, and ask your partner to guess.

— ________ is the ________?
— It's ____________________________.
— ________ can I get there?
— ______________________________
______________________________.

Q: Where is the starting point?
A: It's __________.

教学时长: 15 mins

教学建议:

1. 语法部分旨在巩固学生对本单元询问地点和描述路线的重点句型的理解与运用。

2. 学生可自行在课前或课后完成。课堂上，学生展示和分享作业。教师可指导学生仔细观察地图，识别出不同的场所，并分析场所之间的位置关系。

3. "Step 1"中指明了起点，学生需根据起点和终点的位置分析出具体线路并完成对话；"Step 2"中未指明起点和终点，学生需根据终点附近的地标和线路提示推断出起点和终点位置，并区分"where"和"how"的用法。

4. 通过练习，教师应确保每位学生都熟悉问路方式、描述地点的方式和指路方式。

思维试纸:

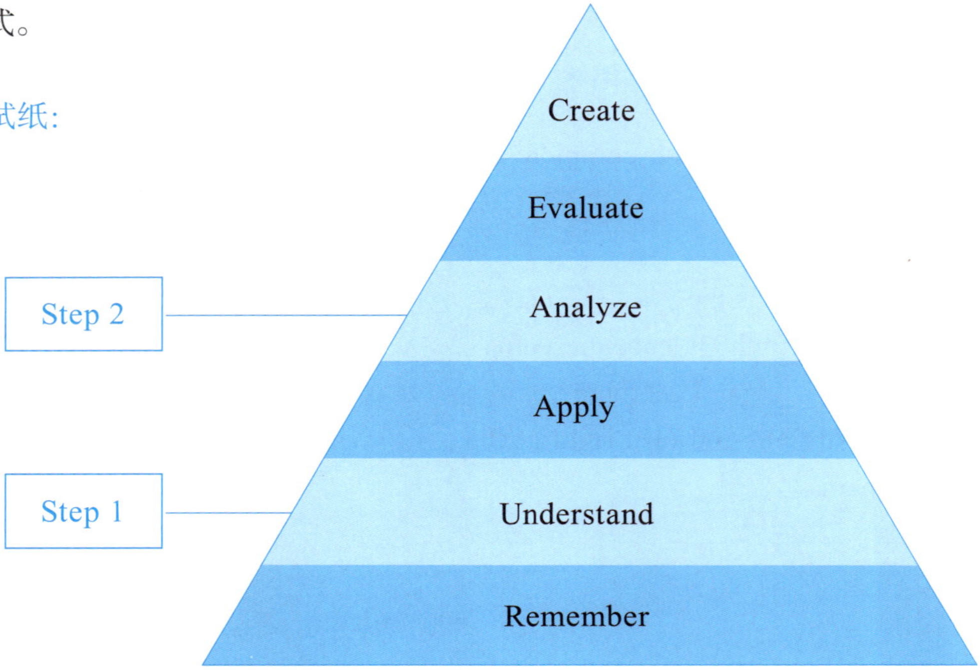

Unit 2 Ways to Go to School

单元导览

单元话题: 交通工具

素材来源: PEP 6A Unit 2 Ways to Go to School

教学目标:

By the end of the lessons, students will be able to

语言目标:

1. **understand** conversations in the textbook and **use** related words and phrases about means of transportation (e.g. bus, plane, subway, taxi, ship, ferry, on foot) in the context;

2. **analyze** different ways to get to given places and **choose** proper destination;

3. **comprehend** the meaning of the story, **analyze** the main content and structure, and **apply** the knowledge and language in the story to writing about their own ideas in another situation.

非语言目标:

1. **choose** proper means of transportation based on the given situation and develop awareness of environment protection/saving money;

2. **predict** proper vehicles used in different places and **understand** cultural differences in other countries;

3. work in groups and collaborate with others to finish tasks related to their daily life about means of transportation;

4. strengthen their higher order thinking skills: **analyzing** and **creating**;

5. **design** travel plan with creative thinking and **judge** with critical thinking.

融思设计

Part One　Listening and Speaking

教学素材: Part A & B　Let's Talk

教学步骤:

Step 1　Listening Comprehension

1. Listen and **write down** the names of speakers on the line according to their means of transportation.

______________　　______________

______________　　______________

2. Listen and decide what you should do (√) and what you shouldn't do (×).

(　　)　　(　　)　　(　　)

3. Try to **write down** the traffic rules in Exercise 2 on the lines. Do you know any other traffic rules?

(1) __________ (2) __________ (3) __________

Other traffic rules: ____

____

Step 2 Preparing before Speaking

There are three different cities you can choose to visit in winter camp for one week, and some information of these places is given below. **Think about** which one you would like to choose, and whether there are more things you want to know about. You can surf on the Internet to collect information, and try to save money when making decisions.

Chongqing–Xi'an

Distance: 687 km

Price: ¥400–1,000 (by plane)
¥281 (by high-speed train)
¥750 (by car, on gas and toll)

Duration: 1.5 hours (by plane)
5 hours (by high-speed train)
9 hours (by car)

Chongqing–Guiyang

Distance: 375 km

Price: no direct flight
¥128 (by high-speed train)
¥400 (by car, on gas and toll)

Duration: 2 hours (by high-speed train)
5 hours (by car)

Chongqing–Kunming

Distance: 842 km

Price: ¥500-1,200 (by plane)
¥341 (by high-speed train)
¥900 (by car, on gas and toll)

Duration: 1.5 hours (by plane)
5 hours (by high-speed train)
10.5 hours (by car)

More Things I Want to Know	
What it is (except distance/price/duration)	What I find

Step 3 Speaking and Sharing

1. Share your choice of winter camp destination with your group members, **talk about** your reasons and decide which city your group will choose.

2. **Finish** a poster with your group members and share in class. You can refer to the following sample and write down the key words. When presenting in class, you need to give a complete speech.

Winter Camp Destination

City: ____________

Means of transportation: ____________

Duration: ____________

Price: ____________

Reasons:

(for choice of city and means of transportation)

(1) ________________________________

(2) ________________________________

(3) ________________________________

(4) ________________________________

Language Kit
(for a complete speech)

Our group chooses __________ to visit in winter camp. We can take _____________ there/go there by __________. It will cost us _________ each person and we will spend _________ hours on the way.

We think it is the best choice because…

教学时长: 1.5 hrs

教学建议:

1. 听力理解环节。

学生可以在学"Part A"和"Part B"两篇对话时分别完成对应的练习。教师播放一遍对话音频,学生完成练习。教师根据学生完成情况可再播放一遍,并订正答案。

2. 表达准备环节。

教师安排学生在学完两篇对话后完成,提醒学生从不同的角度思考并选择心目中最佳目的地和对应的交通方式。另外,教师可以根据情况,启发学生从现实生活的角度考虑问题,比如选择自驾去目的城市虽然耗时长、价格不低,但是一辆车可以坐多位乘客,就可以减少单人消费。除了给出的信息外,教师也可以鼓励学生在表格中填入他们想要知道的其他信息,并借助网络搜索找到相关内容。

3. 表达与分享环节。

(1)教师检查学生课前完成口语准备的情况。

(2)学生四人一组,分享选择的目的地和交通方式,解释原因,并以小组为单位选出本组公认的最佳目的地及对应的交通方式。

(3)小组合作完成本组的海报,可以参考示例中的相关要素。教师可提醒学生只用在海报中填入关键词,而在班级分享时需要组词成句,需参考"Language Kit"中给出的句型呈献完整的演讲。在解释做出选择的原因时,学生可从目的地的选择(如距离远近、冬季天气等)和交通方式的选择(价格、耗时、便利性等)两方面进行思考。

思维试纸:

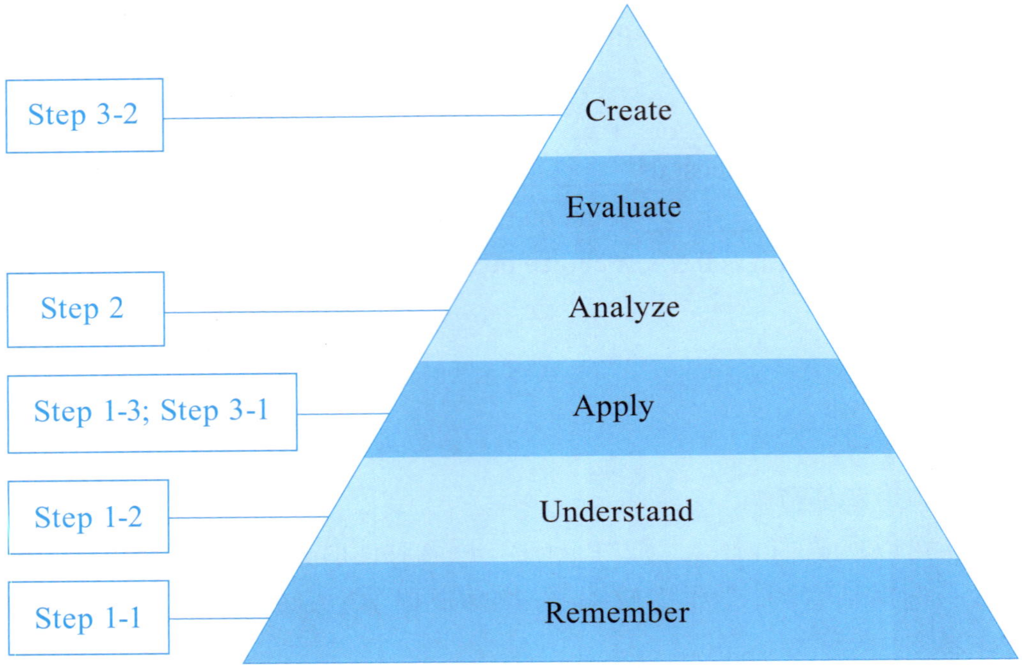

Part Two　Reading and Writing

教学素材: Part B　Read and Write;

Part C　Story Time

教学步骤:

Step 1　Preparation before Reading

1. Do you know where the following cities are? You can search on the Internet and try to **find** them on the world map. Then **talk about** what you know with your classmates.

Cities: Munich（慕尼黑）

Alaska（阿拉斯加）

Jiangxi（江西）

Papa Westray（帕帕韦斯特雷岛）

2. Read the title "Different Ways to Go to School", and **predict** how the students in above cities will go to school in winter. If possible, you can also think about reasons why they may go to school in these ways.

(1) Students in Munich may go to school ________________
because ________________________________.
(2) Students in Alaska may go to school ________________
because ________________________________.
(3) Students in Jiangxi may go to school ________________
because ________________________________.
(4) Students in Papa Westray may go to school ____________
because ________________________________.

Step 2 Reading Comprehension

1. Read "Read and Write" and **match** countries with the means of transportation that children usually take there. In some places, you may choose two different means of transportation.

Munich, Germany	Jiangxi, China	Alaska, USA	Papa Westray, Scotland
on foot	by sled	by plane	by ferry

2. Read "Read and Write" and **decide** wheather the following statements are true (T) or false (F).

______ (1) Children in Alaska go to school by sled only because it is fast.
______ (2) Children in China go to school by ferry every day.
______ (3) Children in Scotland choose the same transportation as those in Germany to go to school.
______ (4) Children in Jiangxi go to school by ferry because there is a river.

3. Read "Story Time" and answer the following questions.

(1) How did they get home?

____

(2) What are the similarities and differences between the UK and China?

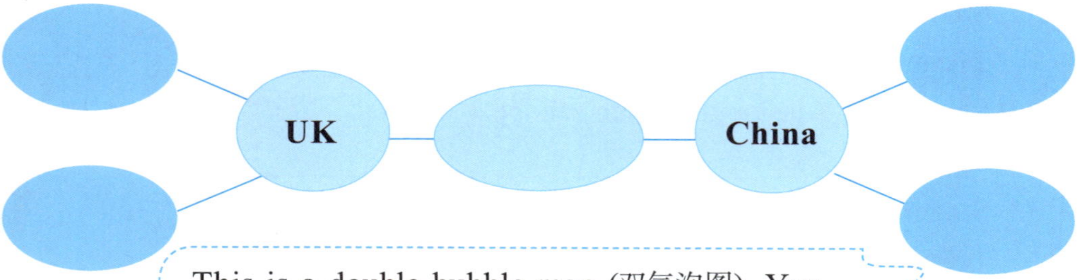

This is a double bubble map (双气泡图). You can write down the similarities of China and the UK in the bubble between them, and put the differences in the bubbles on both sides.

Step 3　Preparation before Writing

1. If you have a chance to choose one city to travel in the next summer holiday (in July), which city would you like to **choose** from the four given cities, and why?

Cities: Beijing, Hainan, Melbourne (墨尔本), Tokyo (东京)

I want to travel in __________, because ______________________________

____

____.

(1) What are the differences of these four cities in geographical location?

e.g. north or south

northern hemisphere or southern hemisphere

(2) What do Beijing and Melbourne look like in July? Are there any differences between the two cities?

2. Complete the following chart to **make** a brief travel plan.

Which city do you choose?	Who do you want to travel with?	How do you go there?	What should you do there?	What shouldn't you do there?

Step 4 Writing and Sharing

Finish the writing based on your travel plan and share with your partner. You can search online for the local customs when you write about what you should/ shouldn't do in your chosen place.

My Travel Plan

I want to visit ________ in the next summer holiday because ____________________________. I plan to go with ___________ and we can ___________ there. There is some advice for travelers that we should pay attention to. For example, _________________
____
____
______________________________________. I believe we will have a good time.

教学时长: 1.5 hrs

教学建议:

1. 读前准备环节。

教师提前给出文章中会出现的四个城市，让学生尝试在地图上找到大概位置，补充相关的地理知识。同时，教师要引导学生根据文章标题预测文章可能讲述的内容，训练学生预测文本的能力。

2. 阅读理解环节。

(1) 学生读完“Read and Write”部分的短文后，教师引导学生根据对文章的理解完成相关练习，检验学生对文章细节的理解（判断题的参考答案：F F F T）。

(2) 学生读完“Story Time”的图文后，教师指导学生完成相应练习。其中第一题旨在检测学生对文章细节的理解，因图文及人物对话错综复杂，学生如不仔细阅读容易答错；第二题旨在训练学生根据文章内容进行归纳分析的能力，此处引入了思维导图中常见的双气泡图（double bubble map）来辅助学生整理相似点和不同点，学生需将相似点填入中间的气泡，不同点分别写在两边的气泡内。

3. 写作准备环节。

(1) 学生需从给出的四个城市中选出在暑假期间旅游最想去的城市，并给出理由。在做出选择时，教师可引导学生思考所列出的问题，比如这四个城市在地理位置上的差异，在七月时北京和墨尔本所处季节是否不同等，培养学生从多角度分析问题的能力。

(2) 在写作前，学生应完成旅行计划的表格。表格内容包含去哪里、和谁去、怎么去、什么能做及什么不能做等要素。学生既可学到制订旅行计划的要素，又可以将其作为写作的大纲（outline），养成先写大纲再成文的习惯。同时，关于什么能做及什么不能做的内容，学生可结合“Read and Write”的拓展内容上网搜索，了解更多当地的习俗。

4. 写作与分享环节。

学生根据写作提示完成写作练习。

思维试纸:

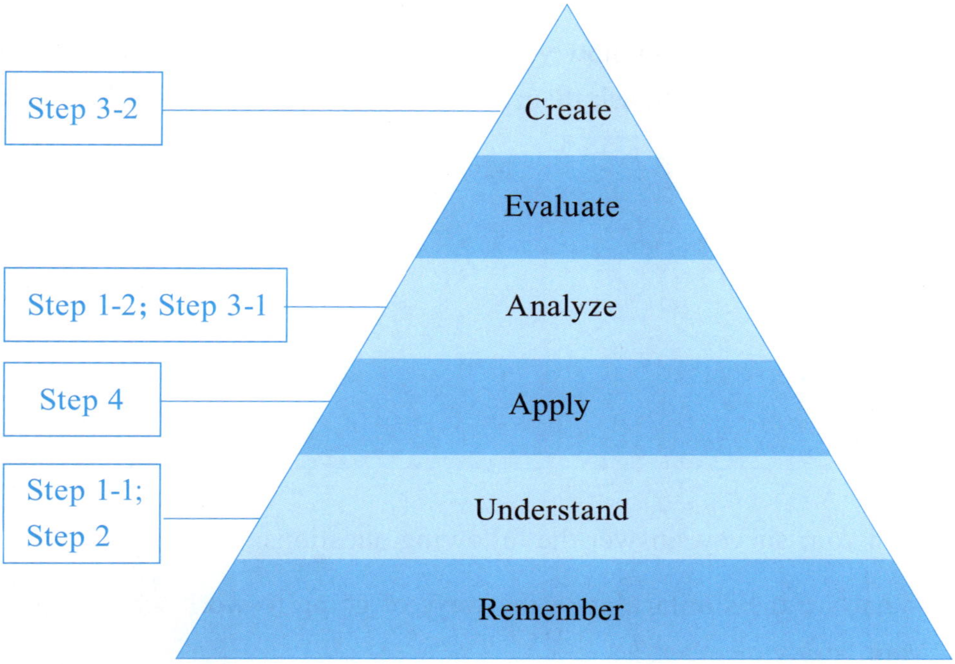

Part Three Vocabulary

教学素材: bus, plane, subway, taxi, bike, ship, ferry, sled, on foot
教学步骤:

Step 1 Guessing

Read the following descriptions and **guess** which means of transportation each one represents?

(1) It has two pedals on each side, and you can ride it to school. ________

(2) It makes several stops on the way, so getting to places can be slow. ________

(3) There is a wing on each side, and you can travel overseas by it. ________

(4) You can use it to slide downhill on a snowy day. ________

(5) You can take it to leave a port. ________

Step 2 Blank-filling

1. **Complete** the survey about how your family members go to work and how you get to school. You need to ask them after class and try to fill all the blanks.

	I	My ________	My ________
usually			
often			
sometimes			
never			

2. Based on your survey, answer the following questions.

(1) What are the similarities in the ways of going to work/school among your family members?

We usually ____.

We seldom ____.

(2) How does your ________ go to work?

She often __________________ because ________________________

____.

(3) How does your ________ go to work?

He usually __________________________________. Besides, he never

____________________________ because ________________________

____.

教学时长: 20 mins

教学建议:

1. 词汇部分主要用于练习，旨在巩固词汇和语法知识。

2. 学生自行在课前或课后完成，教师批改。

3. 本单元词汇部分主要练习了交通工具和表示频率的单词，为加强所学词汇和现实生活的关联性，"Step 2" 首先需要学生采访家庭成员完成问卷调查，并结合实际生活情况思考为什么会经常使用某种交通工具(比如经常乘地铁,因为不会堵车),以及如果有的交通工具绝对不会使用的原因(比如不会乘雪橇,因为不下雪)。

思维试纸:

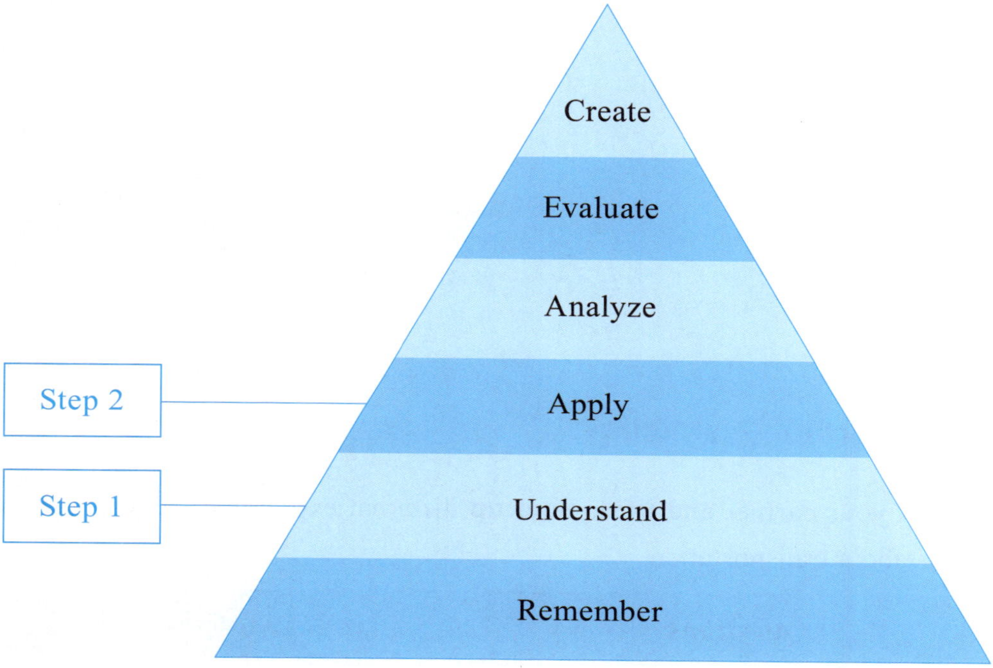

Part Four Grammar

教学素材: How do you go/come/get to...?
by subway/bus/bike/car/plane/taxi/train/ferry/sled
on foot

教学步骤:

Step 1 Self-checking

1. Which sentences are grammatically correct? Read and **find** out.

A. What do you go to school?
B. How do you come to school?
C. How do you go to school?
D. How do you get to school?

2. Read and **match**.

Step 2 Further Practicing

Work with your partner and try to **sum up** different expressions to ask and answer questions about transportation.

Questions	Answers
How do you go to school? You can also say: __________ __________ __________ __________ __________	I go to school by __________/on __________. You can also say: __________ __________ __________ __________ __________

教学时长: 15 mins

教学建议:

1. 语法部分旨在巩固学生对重点句型的运用。本单元要求学生运用 “how” 开头的特殊疑问句询问交通方式及区分介词 “by” 和 “on”。

2. 学生可自行在课前或课后完成。课堂上, 学生展示和分享作业。

3. 学生在 “Step 1” 复习了 “how” 引导的问句及区分了 “by” 和 “on” 的搭配后, 在 “Step 2” 中, 教师应鼓励学生尽可能地使用不同的表达询问和回答相关问题。如除了问 “How do you go to school?” 之外, 还可以用 “How do you come/get to school?”, 在回答时, 除了用 “I go to school by bus”, 也可以用 “I take a bus to school” 等表达。

思维试纸:

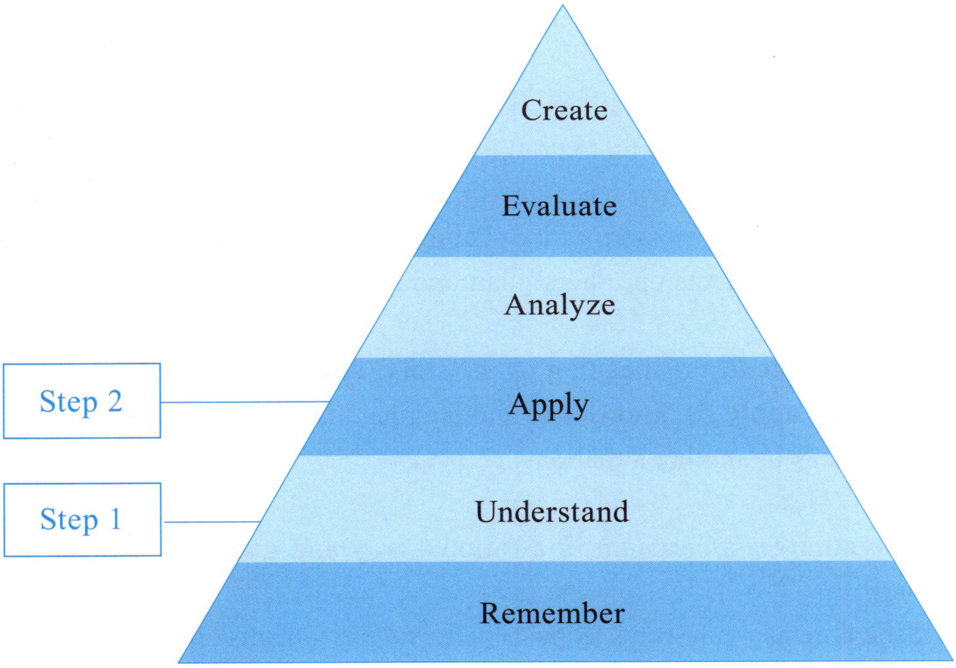

Unit 3 My Weekend Plan

单元导览

单元话题: 周末计划

素材来源: PEP 6A Unit 3 My Weekend Plan

教学目标:

By the end of the lessons, students will be able to

语言目标:

1. **understand** conversations in the textbook and **ask** others' future plan (e.g. What are you/they going to do this morning/evening?);

2. **introduce** their own schedule (e.g. draw some pictures, see a film, buy a comic book, have an art lesson, go ice-skating, visit grandparents, etc.) in detail;

3. **make** comments on others' plan and **give** suggestions to make it more reasonable;

4. **comprehend** the meaning of the story, **analyze** the main content and structure, and **apply** the knowledge and language in the story to writing about their own ideas in another situation.

非语言目标:

1. **evaluate** a week plan in a rational way and give suggestions when necessary;

2. explore as many ways as possible to **solve** problems and achieve goals;

3. work in groups and collaborate with others to finish tasks related to their daily life about week plan;

4. strengthen their higher order thinking skills: **analyzing**, **evaluating** and **creating**;

5. **make** conversations with creative thinking and **judge** with critical thinking.

融思设计

Part One Listening and Speaking

教学素材: Part A & B Let's Talk
教学步骤:

Step 1 Listening Comprehension

Listen carefully and **complete** the following chart.

Who	Where	What	When
Mike		see a film	(1) ________
Sarah	Renmin Park	(2) ________	tomorrow
John	(3) ________	see a film	next Wednesday → ________

Step 2 Preparation before Speaking

1. Think about what you want to do this week, and how you can **remember** these things.

2. **Write down** your plans for this week. You should write at least 3 things on the calendar.

________'s Week Plan

	Monday	Tuesday	Wednesday	Thursday	Friday	Saturday & Sunday
Morning						
Afternoon						
Evening						

Language Kit

draw some pictures
look for some beautiful leaves
see a film (about...)/go to the cinema
buy a comic book (about...)
have an art lesson
go ice-skating
wash clothes
make a snowman
go for a picnic
visit my grandparents
go to the supermarket

Step 3 Speaking and Sharing

Role play: Share your week plan with your partner, and then **make** a conversation and present in class.

Tip: In the conversation, you can ask each other's plan first and then **comment on** the plans and give advice.

Language Kit

ask for plans:

- What are you going to do on Monday/ Monday afternoon?
- I'm going to...
- What about you?
- When/Where are you going to...?

comment or give advice:

- Why not...?
- How about...?

教学时长: 1.5 hrs

教学建议:

1. 听力理解环节。

(1) 教师可把 “Part A” 和 “Part B” 两篇对话结合起来教学, 教师播放一遍对话音频, 学生完成练习。教师提醒学生听音过程中需要注意表格中关于 “where” “what” “when” 的相关信息。教师根据学生完成情况可再播放一遍, 并订正答案。

(2) 教师引导学生注意约翰 (John) 的计划中具体时间有变化并讨论约翰 (John) 改变时间的原因, 帮助学生认识计划可能存在不合理时需要做出适当改变的情况。

表格中应填入的是: tomorrow; have an art lesson; cinema; next Tuesday

2. 表达准备环节。

学生在学完两篇对话后完成, 在填表时可以参考 “Language Kit” 提供的短语。

3. 表达与分享环节。

(1) 教师检查学生课前完成表格情况。

(2) 两人一组, 根据自己所填的表格内容, 参考课文和 “Language Kit” 提供的句型互相询问各自的周计划, 并针对不合理或者有待改进的地方提出建议, 巩固练习相关句型, 也培养学生分析、评价的能力。

思维试纸:

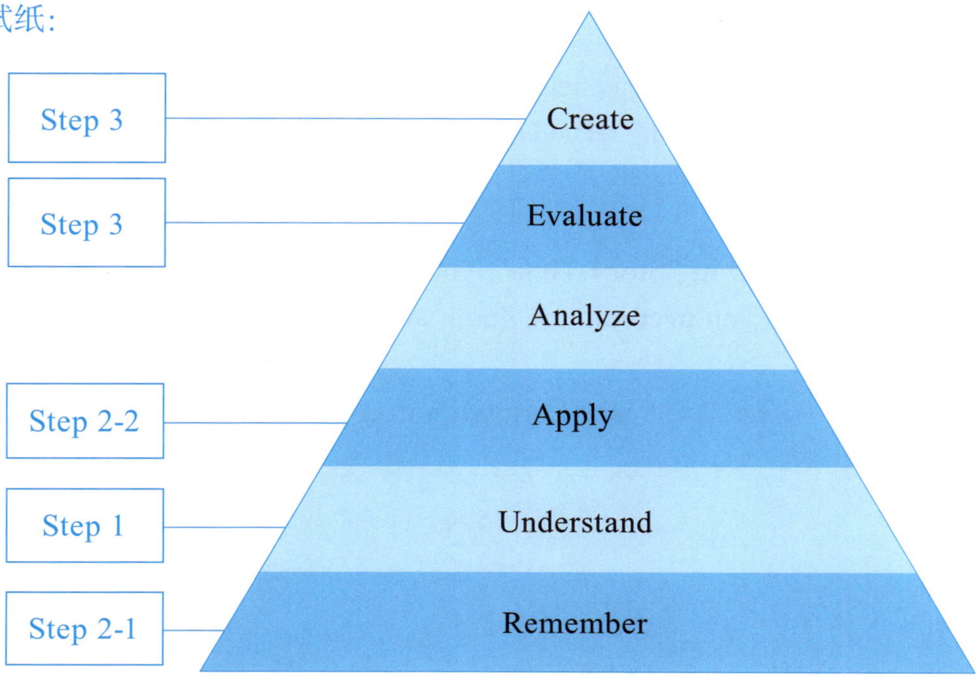

Part Two　Reading and Writing

教学素材: Part C　Story Time

教学步骤:

Step 1　Preparation before Reading

1. If you have a swimming test in your PE lesson at the end of this semester, how many ways can you **think about** to learn swimming?

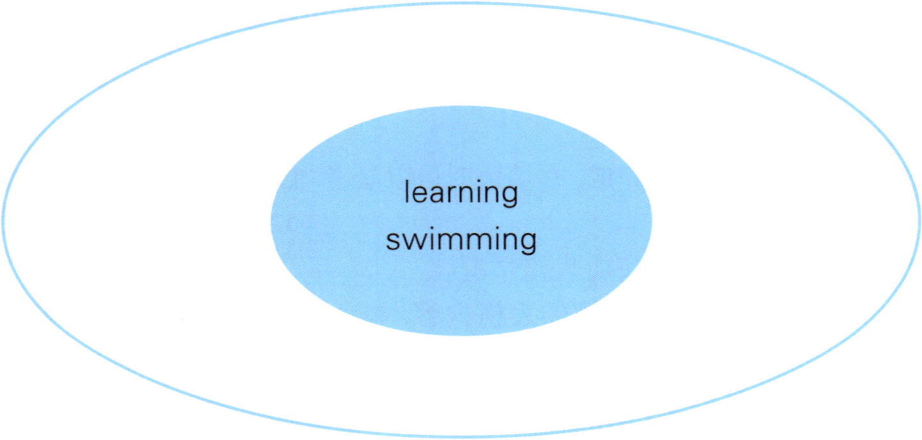

Circle map (圆圈图) is helpful to generate ideas. You can write down anything related to the topic in the circle.

2. From the pictures in “Story Time”, you can find that Zoom is also learning swimming. Can you **predict** how Zoom learns swimming?

e.g. Zoom may learn swimming by ____________
____.

Step 2 Reading Comprehension

Read the story and **finish** the following map. You need to find what methods Zoom uses to learn swimming.

Zoom learns swimming by ______________________.

and →

Zoom learns swimming by ______________________.

↓ the result

____

↓ the result

____

Step 3 Preparation before Writing

1. From Zoom's example, we know there is more than one method to learn a skill. Now, if you are invited to share your experience of learning English, what methods can you **think about**? Work with your group members and finish the first row of the following map.

I learn English by ________________.

I learn English by ________________.

I learn English by ________________.

↓

____
____

↓

____
____

↓

____
____

2. Exchange with another group, and **write down** comments or **give** advice for each method on the second row of the above map.

Step 4 Writing and Sharing

Read comments or advice from the other group and work with your group members to **finish** the following writing.

> There are three ways to learn English. First, you can ____________________________________. Besides, you can also ____________________________. Finally, ________________________________. Among them, ____ can be very helpful. However, ____ doesn't work for everyone.

教学时长: 1 hr

教学建议:

1. 读前准备环节。

(1) 此处引入了思考图(thinking map)中的圆圈图(circle map), 可以帮助学生针对给定的主题展开联想, 进行头脑风暴, 并整合思路。教师不限制学生在圆圈中记录想法的形式, 可以是关键词、短语, 也可以是简笔画等, 只要是和主题 "learning swimming" 相关的即可。

(2) 教师引导学生根据文章配图预测文章可能讲述的内容, 训练学生预测文本的能力。

2. 阅读理解环节。

学生读完短文后, 教师引导学生根据对文章的理解完成图表, 检查学生对文章逻辑的理解。图表中 "Zoom" 所用游泳方法可填入 "by watching TV/jumping in the swimming pool", 而在两种方法对应的效果部分, 学生可用自己的语言表达, 只要体现出前一种未成功而后一种成功的区别即可。

3. 写作准备环节。

(1) 从学习游泳迁移到学习其他技能, 以学习英语为例, 学生以小组为单位, 完成图表中第一排, 即根据个人经验归纳出学习英语可以使用的方法。

(2) 小组和另一组交换图表，针对第一排已经填入的内容，互相评价每一种方式，并在图表中第二排写下评论或给出建议（可以从实际效果、实践起来的难易程度等方面），训练学生分析、评价的能力。

4. 写作与分享环节。

各组拿回各自的表格，仔细阅读其他组同学给的评论或建议，小组合作根据写作提示完成写作练习。

思维试纸:

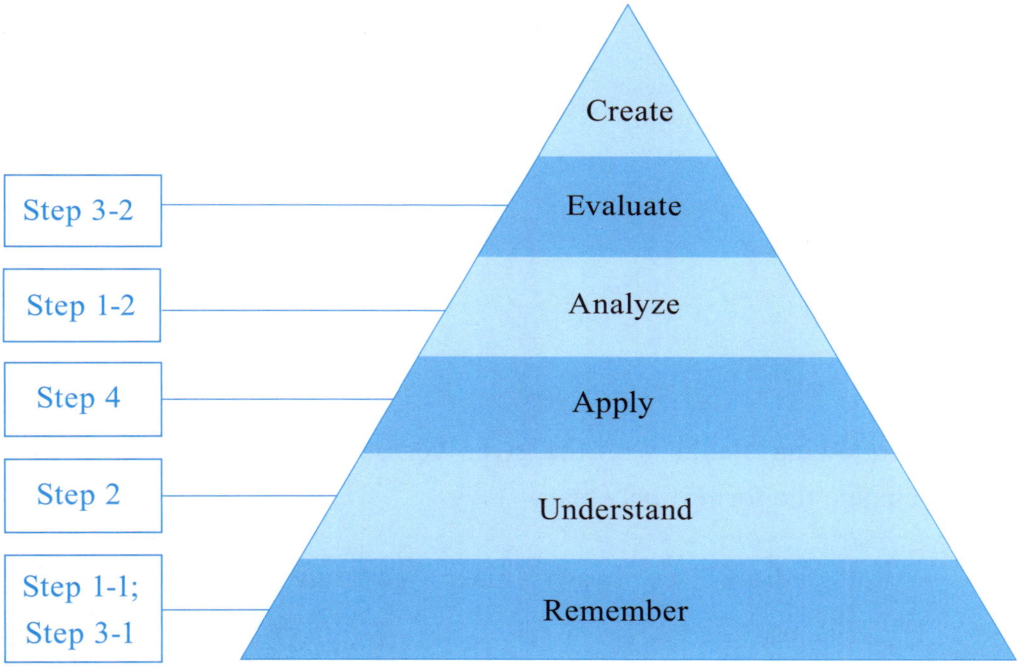

Part Three　Vocabulary

教学素材: comic book, word book, dictionary, postcard, visit grandparents, take a trip, go to the supermarket, see a film, go to the cinema, draw some pictures

教学步骤：

Step 1 Word-making

Make words with the letters given in the bubble. Each letter can be used more than once. Try to write down as many words you learn in this unit as you can and share with your partner.

Step 2 Blank-filling

Fill in the following blanks with the given verbs. Each word can be used only once, and change the form if necessary.

draw see wash make go buy

(1) I'm going to __________ a film tonight.

(2) He is going to __________ some pictures in the park tomorrow.

(3) We plan to __________ the latest comic book this week.

(4) — I want to __________ ice-skating next week.

— How about __________ a snowman with us?

(5) — What is your mom doing now?

— She __________ clothes.

教学时长: 20 mins

教学建议:

1. 词汇部分主要用于练习, 旨在巩固词汇和语法知识。

2. 学生自行在课前或课后完成, 教师批改或让学生在课堂上分享展示, 及时纠错。

3. "Step 1" 为开放式练习, 学生根据所提供的字母可任意拼写出本单元所学的单词, 并和同伴分享, 看谁写得又多又准确, 教师也可以要求学生同时写出单词的中文意思。

4. "Step 2" 练习中每个动词只能使用一次, 教师可以提醒学生填入动词时注意动词的形式是否需要进行变化。

参考答案:

(1) see (2) draw (3) buy (4) go (5) making (6) is washing

思维试纸:

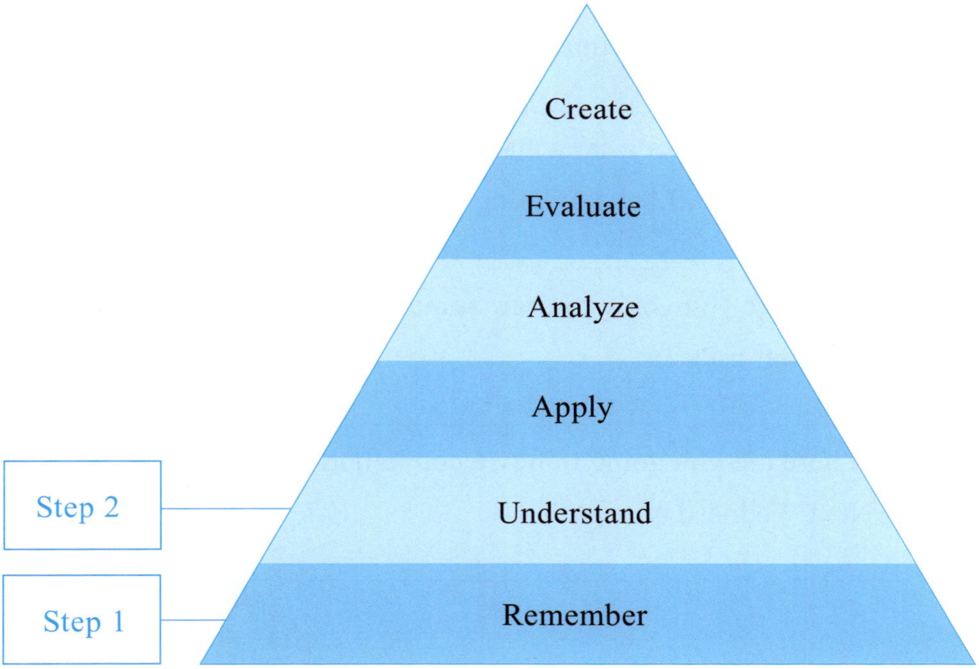

Part Four　Grammar

教学素材: What are you/they going to do?/What is… going to do?
I'm/He is/She is/They are going to…
What about you?
When are you going to…?
Where are you going to…?

教学步骤:

Step 1　Self-checking

There is a mistake in each sentence below. **Underline** the mistake and write down the correct form.

(1) John are going to visit his grandparents tomorrow.

____

(2) We is going to see a film tonight.

____

(3) —We plan to make a snowman this weekend. Let's go together!
—Sorry, I can't. I have to doing my homework.

____

(4) —When are you going to draw some pictures?
—In Renmin Park.

____

(5) —Where are you going to buy a comic book?
—Next Wednesday.

____

Step 2 Fruther Practicing

Write a dialogue between John and Amy. You need to use all information given in the box, and you can add more plots. Share your dialogue with your partner and ask for comments.

Who: John, Amy
Where: bookstore
When: this afternoon, next Monday
What: buy a comic book, see a film

John: ______________________________
Amy: ______________________________
John: ______________________________
Amy: ______________________________
John: ______________________________
Amy: ______________________________
John: ______________________________
Amy: ______________________________
...

教学时长: 20 mins
教学建议:

1. 语法部分旨在巩固学生对重点句型的运用。本单元要求学生运用"what""where""when"引导的特殊疑问句询问近期的计划安排。

2. 学生可自行在课前或课后完成,教师批改或让学生互相批改,并及时纠错。

3. "Step 1"旨在让学生判断出句子中错误的部分,并进行改正,错误的部分也是学生在应用时的易错点。

4.“Step 2”要求学生根据给出的信息编写情景对话，给出的要素也是询问计划中常见的“who”“where”“when”“what”几大要素。编写对话是开放式练习，学生需要在对话中包含所有指定的信息，并且在逻辑上合理，比如给出的时间和事件不止一条，对话中就必然包含不止一项计划；学生也可以根据个人需要增加情节。

思维试纸：

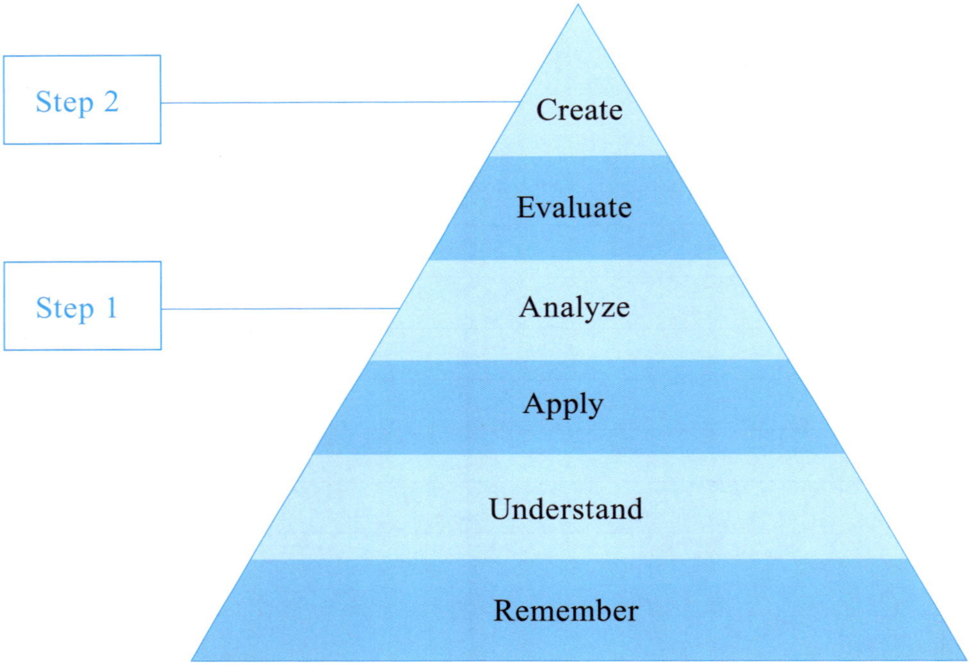

Unit 4 I Have a Pen Pal

单元导览

单元话题: 爱好

素材来源: PEP 6A Unit 4 I Have a Pen Pal

教学目标:

By the end of the lessons, students will be able to

语言目标:

1. **ask** others' hobbies and **introduce** their own hobbies (e.g. collect stamps, play games, climb mountains, read stories, listen to music, etc.) as well as **connect** hobbies with corresponding behaviors;

2. **understand** conversations in the textbook and **discuss** places where they can do the things they like;

3. **summarize** the main features of simple present tense and **apply** the rules in conversations;

4. **comprehend** the meaning of the story, **analyze** the main content and structure, and **apply** the knowledge and language in the story to writing about their own ideas in another situation.

非语言目标:

1. build up deeper understanding of the classmates and respect others' interests;

2. work in groups to finish tasks related to their daily life about hobbies;

3. strengthen their higher order thinking skills: **analyzing**, **evaluating** and **creating**;

4. **design** a new ending for a story by using creative thinking and **judge** with critical thinking.

融思设计

Part One　Listening and Speaking

教学素材: Part A　Let's Talk

教学步骤:

Step 1　Preparation before Listening

Look at the picture in the textbook, **guess** the answers to the following questions and give your reasons.

(1) Where does he live?

____

(2) What is he doing?

____

(3) What is his hobby?

____

Step 2　Listening Comprehension

Listen to the conversation, and **circle** Peter's hobbies.

feeding cows　　climbing mountains　　reading

playing kung fu　　swimming　　playing the pipa

watching kung fu movies　　teaching Chinese songs

Step 3 Preparation before Speaking

1. **Observe** the pictures below and **guess** what might be these people's hobbies.

(1) ______________

(2) ______________

(3) ______________

(4) ______________

(5) ______________

(6) ______________

2. Can you try to **put** these hobbies into different groups? You can use the chart given below, or design your own chart in the box.

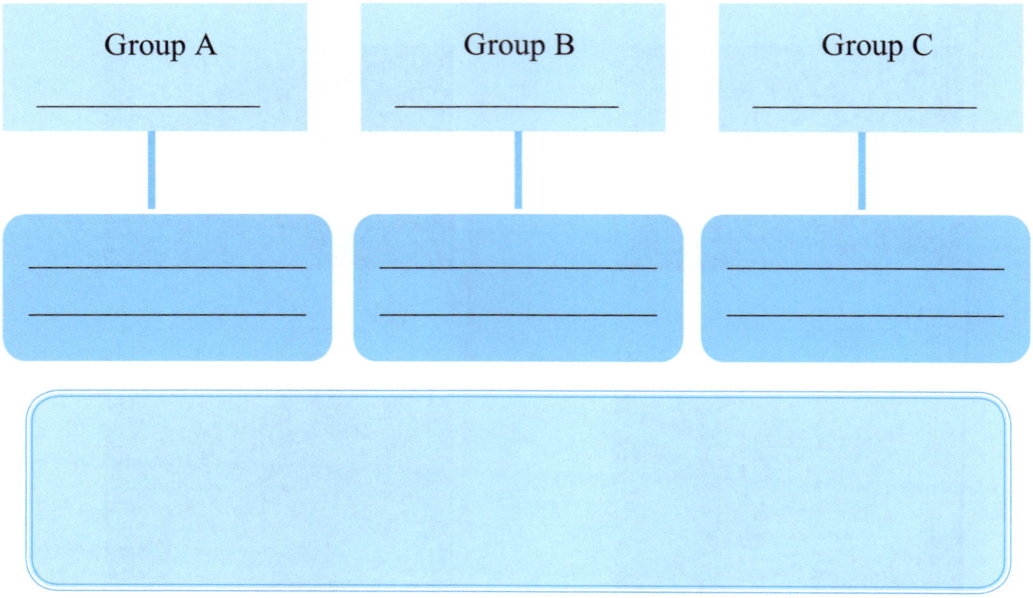

Step 4 Speaking and Sharing

1. Share your design with your partner and check if you have different ways to **classify** the hobbies.

2. **Interview** your group members about their hobbies, and **put** their hobbies into different groups.

教学时长: 1 hr

教学建议:

1. 听前准备环节。

教师让学生根据 “Let’s Talk” 部分的配图预测对话涉及的内容，训练学生在听前结合已有信息和生活经验来预测听力内容的能力。

2. 听力理解环节。

教师播放一遍对话音频，学生完成练习。教师根据学生完成情况可再播放一遍，并订正答案。参考答案如下:

feeding cows　climbing mountains　reading
playing kung fu　swimming　playing the pipa
watching kung fu movies　teaching Chinese songs

3. 表达准备环节。

(1) 教师给出不同图片，图片中的人物在做不同的事，学生根据人物正在做的事来判断他们可能的爱好，并写在横线上。

(2) 学生将所填写的爱好进行分类，练习中给出了一个简易的树状图作为参考，学生也可以自行设计，只要有自己的标准，逻辑合理即可。

4. 表达与分享环节。

(1) 学生与同伴分享所设计的图表，了解可能存在的不同分类方式。

(2) 以小组为单位，学生用所学句型询问组员爱好，进行记录，并且用分类的方式进行汇总。

思维试纸：

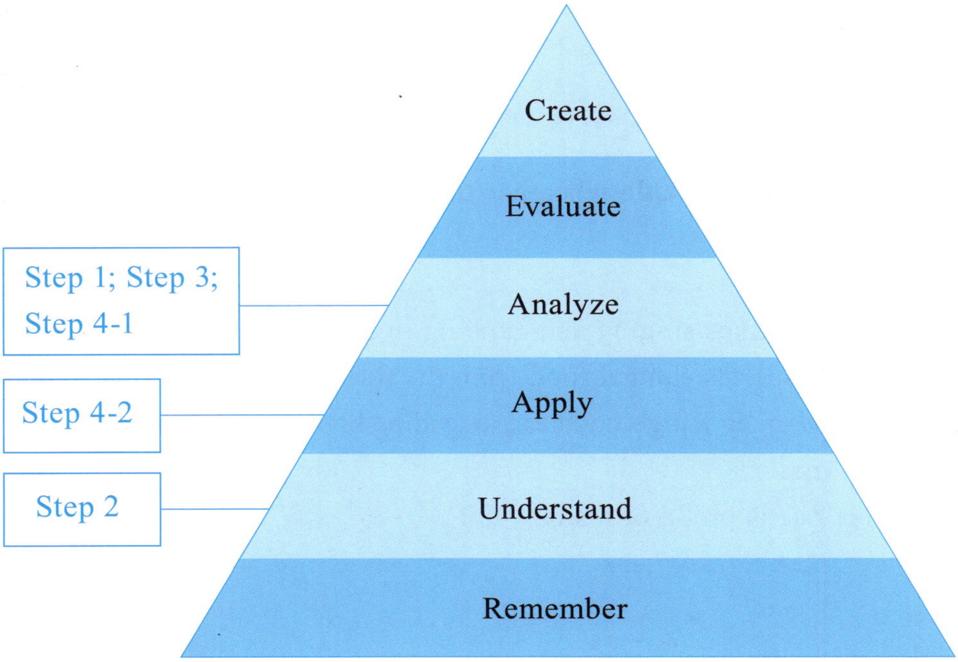

Part Two Reading and Writing

教学素材: Part C Story Time

教学步骤:

Step 1 Preparation before Reading

Look at pictures in the story. **Guess** what Zac and Monkey King may like and what story may happen between them.

Zac's hobby might be ________________.

Monkey King's hobby might be ________________.

↓

What may happen between them?

____

____

Step 2 Reading Comprehension

1. Read the story and **decide** wheather the following statements are true (T) or false (F).

____ (1) Zac likes singing and dancing in front of other animals.

____ (2) Squirrels can get food from the forest for free.

____ (3) Monkey King's hobbies are reading books and listening to music.

____ (4) Zac is proud of his new tail.

2. **Make** comments and fill in the blanks.

The Monkey King likes __________ and he doesn't like __________, so he ____________________. I agree/disagree with his behavior because __________ ____________________.

Step 3 Preparation before Writing

Interview your group members to know their hobbies and **find out** which hobby is most popular.

Names	Hobbies

Ranking of Hobbies

No. 1 ____________________

No. 2 ____________________

No. 3 ____________________

No. 4 ____________________

No. 5 ____________________

Step 4 Writing and Sharing

Based on your interview, **write down** the hobbies of your group members.

In my group, ________ likes ________________________,
and ________ loves ________________________________.
_______ (hobby) is __________________ and ___________
is my favorite thing. Among them, ____________________
is the popular choice.

教学时长: 1.5 hrs

教学建议:

1. 读前准备环节。

教师让学生根据图片信息预测文章可能讲述的内容，训练学生预测文本的能力。

2. 阅读理解环节。

(1) 学生读完短文后，教师引导学生根据对文章的理解完成相关练习，检验学生对文章大意和部分细节的理解(判断题的参考答案：T F F T)。

(2) 教师应引导学生练习简要概括文本的能力，以及结合文章内容对文中人物行为做出评价的能力。

3. 写作准备环节。

(1) 以小组为单位，学生互相采访组员，询问各自的兴趣爱好并进行记录。

(2) 学生将采访所得信息进行整理，以自己的方式绘制出本组的爱好排行榜，分析得出本组同学的共同兴趣。

4. 写作与分享环节。

基于采访内容，学生根据写作提示完成写作练习。

思维试纸:

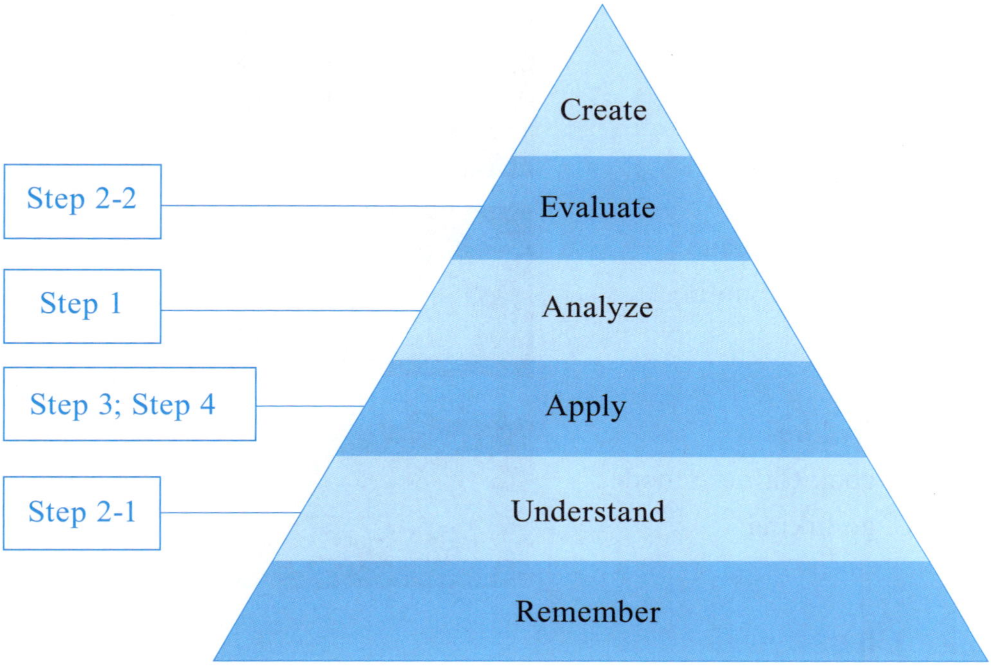

Part Three　Vocabulary

教学素材: fly kites, play sports, climb mountains, listen to music, watch TV, play the pipa, draw cartoons, sing, dance, read stories, play football, do kung fu, cook Chinese food, do word puzzles, go hiking

教学步骤:

Step 1　Multiple Choice

Choose the phrase to match each given picture.

(　　) 1. A. sing a song
B. have a dance class
C. read a story

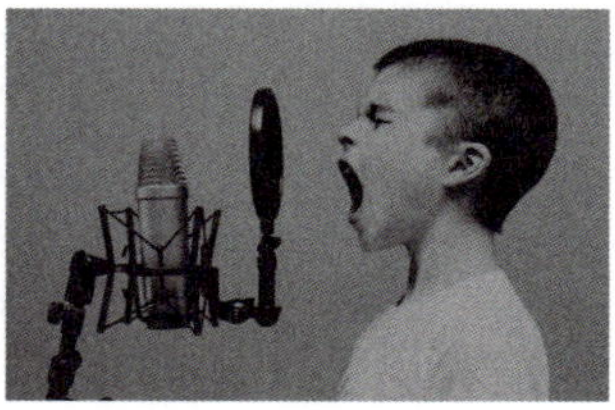

(　　) 2. A. watch TV
B. draw cartons
C. listen to music

(　　) 3. A. play the pipa
B. play the piano
C. play the violin

(　　) 4. A. fly kites
B. cook Chinese food
C. go hiking

Step 2　Classifying

Divide the following phrases into four categories, and only write down the Chinese meanings of these phrases on the lines.

climb mountains	play football	play the pipa
do word puzzles	study English	play the guitar
listen to music	play ping-pong	go hiking
play tennis	read stories	go fishing
play the piano		

(1) ______________________________
(2) ______________________________
(3) ______________________________
(4) ______________________________

教学时长: 15 mins

教学建议:

1. 词汇部分主要用于练习，旨在巩固词汇和语法知识。

2. 学生自行在课前或课后完成，教师批改。

3. 课堂上，教师带领学生总结存在的问题和解决办法，注重引导学生识记和辨析本单元重点短语。

4. "Step 1" 检测学生对短语的理解。"Step 2" 训练学生建立标准，对短语进行分类归纳和识记的能力，此处的标准并不唯一。教师可以让学生互相介绍和解释分类的依据，言之成理即可，可以参考的标准如下（学生作答时需写出中文意思，此处只是方便教师对照查看）：

(1) climb mountains, go hiking, go fishing
(2) play football, play tennis, play ping-pong
(3) play the pipa, play the piano, play the guitar, listen to music
(4) do word puzzles, study English, read stories

思维试纸:

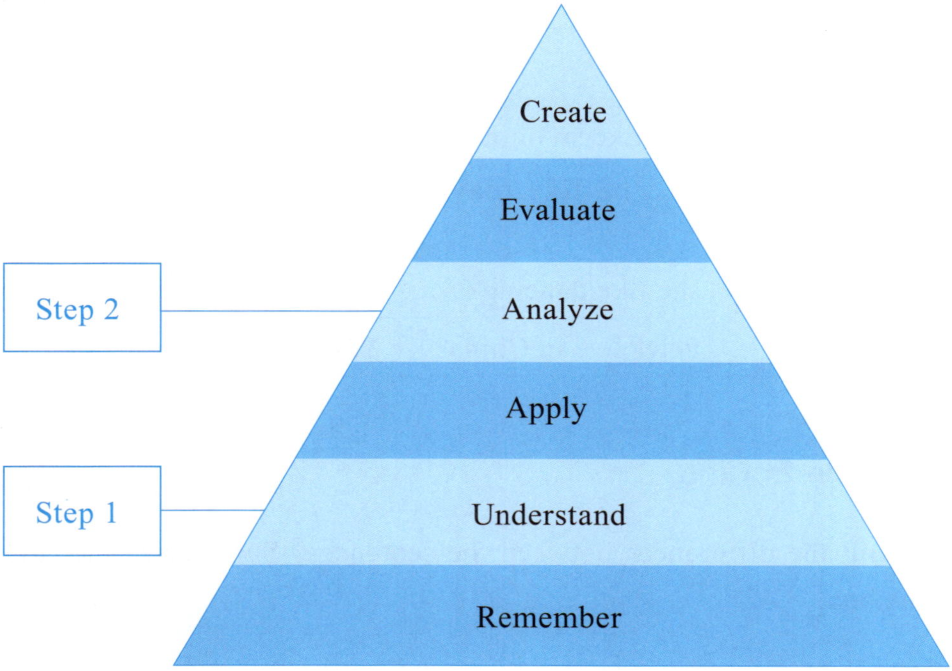

Part Four　Grammar

教学素材: — What do you like?
— I like...

— What are his hobbies?
— He likes...

— Does he like...?
— Yes, he does.

教学步骤:

Step 1　Self-checking

Complete the following chart to make right sentences.

I	What ________ you like?	What ________ your hobby?
He	What ________ he like?	What are his ________?
She	What ________ she like?	What ________ her hobby?
Peter	What ________ Peter like?	What are ________ hobbies?

I	________ you like swimming?	Yes, I ________.
He	________ he like playing basketball?	No, he ________ ________.
She	________ she like dancing?	No, ________ ________.
Peter	________ Peter live in China?	Yes, ________ ________.

Step 2　Rule-finding

Can you **find** the differences between the sentences? Summarize the rules you find in the box.

教学时长: 20 mins

教学建议:

1. 语法部分旨在巩固学生对重点句型的运用。本单元要求学生掌握运用询问爱好的句型。

2. 学生可自行在课前或课后完成,教师及时纠错。

3. 在完成"Step 1"填写表格的练习后,"Step 2"旨在让学生总结他们发现的规律,可以是对询问爱好的句型进行总结,也可以是对第三人称单数或者物主代词使用规律的总结,教师可以引导学生注意观察"Step 1"的表格,并鼓励学生举更多例子来验证规律。

思维试纸:

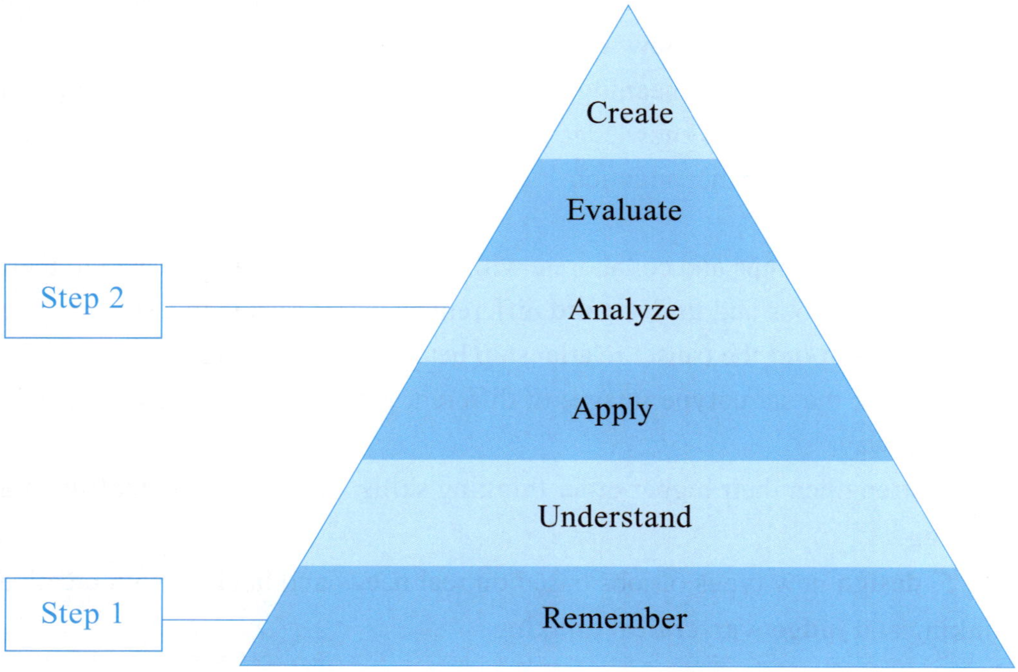

Unit 5　What Does He Do?

单元导览

单元话题: 工作与职业
素材来源: PEP 6A Unit 5 What Does He Do?
教学目标:

By the end of the lessons, students will be able to

语言目标:

1. **comprehend** the listening material and catch specific information like “who” “what” “where” and “how”;

2. develop their communicative ability by **interviewing** each other;

3. know how to **use** sentence patterns like “Where does he work?” “How does he go to work?” and answer these questions by using “He works at/in...” “He goes to work by...” and **review** words about jobs learned in this unit;

4. **comprehend** the meaning of the story, **analyze** the main content and structure, and **apply** the knowledge and language in the story to writing about their own ideas in another situation.

非语言目标:

1. work in groups and collaborate with others to finish tasks related to their daily life about jobs and **understand** different elements related to a specific job;

2. **understand** the causal relationship between hobbies and jobs;

3. break the stereotype images of different jobs and **create** new images in a rational way;

4. strengthen their higher order thinking skills: **analyzing**, **evaluating** and **creating**;

5. **design** new types of jobs based on real needs and hobbies with creative thinking and **judge** with critical thinking.

融思设计

Part One Listening and Speaking

教学素材: Part B Let's Talk
教学步骤:

Step 1 Preparation before Listening

1. Look at the picture in the textbook, and **write down** any questions you want to ask about the conversation between two speakers.

Questions

e.g. What are they talking about?

____

____

____

____

____

2. Invite your partner to **guess** answers to the above questions, and then write down the answers.

Answers

e.g. They are talking about a man's job.

____

____

____

____

____

Step 2　Listening Comprehension

Listen to the conversation and **fill in** the chart.

Who is this person?	
What is his job?	
Where does he work?	
How does he go to work?	
What can we learn from this person?	

Step 3　Preparation before Speaking

Interview your family member to know their jobs, and then complete the following survey.

Jobs of My Family Members	
Who is this person?	
What is his/her job?	
Where does he/she work?	
How does he/she go to work?	
What is this job about?	
How long does he/she work every day?	
I think…	

Step 4 Speaking and Sharing

Share your survey with your partner and make a conversation to **ask** jobs of each other's family members. You can refer to the following questions or those in the survey.

Language Kit

What does… do?

What is his/her job?

Where does he/she work?

How does he/she go to work?

What do you think about this job?

What can we learn from him/her?

hrs

教

听前准备环节。

教师让学生根据配图预测对话涉及的内容，训练学生在听前结合已有信息和生活经验来预测听力内容的能力。教师可以让学生先根据配图写下他们想要知道的相关问题，完成后和同伴交换并互相回答问题。学生听完后可以验证所听内容是否和自己的预测一致。

2. 听力理解环节。

(1) 教师播放一遍对话音频，学生完成练习。教师根据学生完成情况可再播放一遍，并订正答案。

(2) 教师引导学生思考问题：如果要了解一个人的职业，有哪些方面是需要了解的？教师可根据学生的回答在黑板上写出相关要素，为后续学生互相采访做铺垫。

3. 表达准备环节。

教师安排学生在课后选择两位家庭成员进行采访，并将获得的信息填入表中。

4. 表达与分享环节。

(1) 教师检查学生课前完成调查采访的情况。

（2）学生两人一组，互相分享采访信息，并参照课文对话、调查表格中的问题和“Language Kit”编对话，询问各自家庭成员的工作信息并进行评价。教师可以引导学生从不同角度正面思考如何回答“What can we learn from him/her?”，也可以请学生在全班表演对话。

思维试纸：

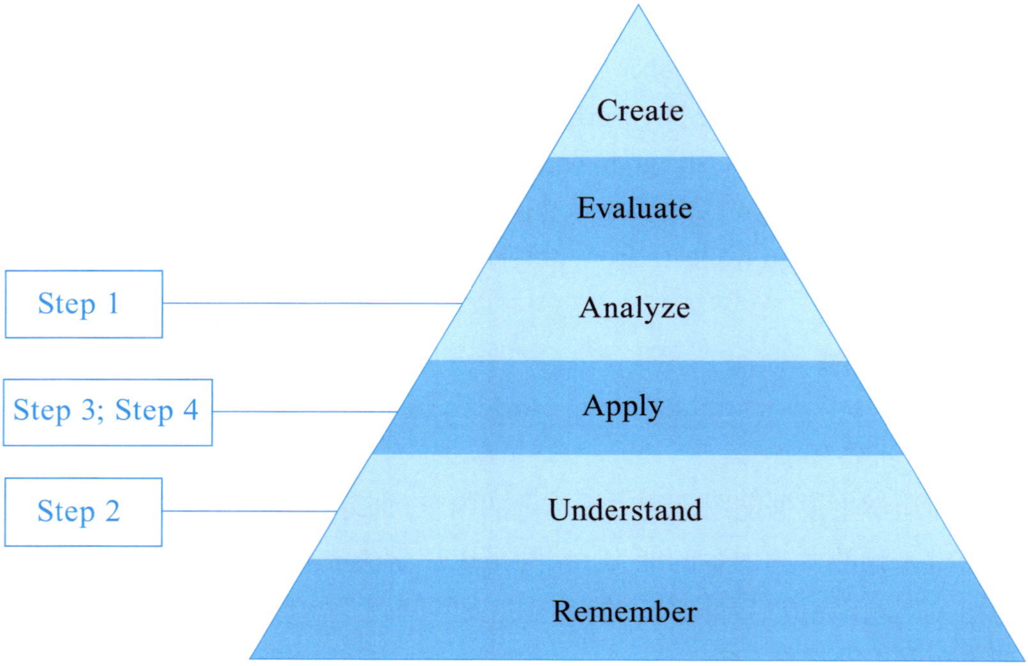

Part Two Reading and Writing

教学素材：Part B Read and Write

教学步骤：

Step 1 Preparation before Reading

There are some different jobs in the box below. **Think about** their similarities and differences, and choose two of them to complete the double bubble map.

PE teacher fisherman scientist coach pilot police officer

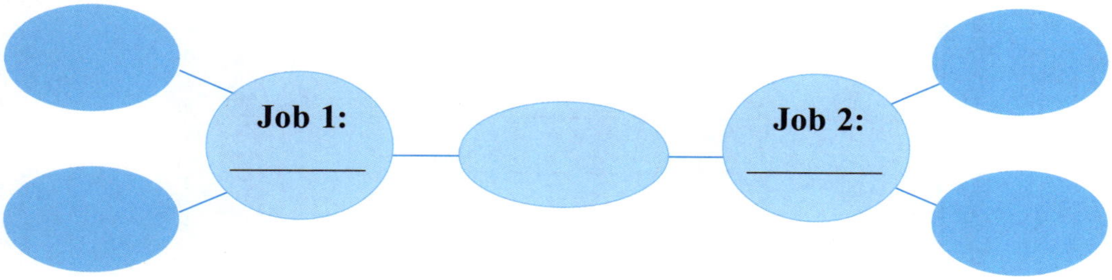

This is a double bubble map. You can write down the similarities of Job 1 and Job 2 in the bubble between them, and put the differences in the bubbles on both sides.

Step 2 Reading Comprehension

1. Read and **match**.

Sarah	football	coach
Hu Bin	computer	PE teacher
Robin	basketball	scientist
	type quickly	secretary
	science	
	ping-pong	
	study hard	
	running	

2. Can you **find** any connection between the middle column and the right column? Write down your ideas.

____

____

____

Step 3 Preparation before Writing

Based on the connection you find in the reading text, think about what you are good at and what you want to do in the future, and then **finish** the following career planning of your own.

My Career Planning	
Name	
Things I like/I'm good at	
Jobs I can do	
Other things to think about	
Final choice	
Things I need to do to get the job	

You may have a lot of hobbies and more than one job you want to do in the future. However, you also need to think about other things, for example, your parents' suggestions and the detailed information about some jobs. Then, you can make a final choice. At last, think about things you need to do to get your dream job.

Step 4 Writing and Sharing

After thinking about your career planning clearly, you can **finish** the writing below and share with your partner.

Language Kit

I like…/I can…

I'm good at…

I want to do…/be… in the future.

However, …

So, I decide to choose… as my dream job.

教学时长: 1 hr

教学建议:

1. 读前准备环节。

教师使用“双气泡图”让学生从给出的不同职业中选出两个进行比较，找出相似点和不同点，检验学生对不同职业具体工作内容的理解，也为阅读文章的相关内容做准备。教师也可鼓励学生根据个人需求增加气泡的个数，从更多方面比较异同。

2. 阅读理解环节。

（1）学生读完短文后，教师引导学生根据对文章的理解完成连线，注意一个人物对应的爱好不止一个。

（2）学生完成连线后，教师引导学生观察中间栏和右边栏的关系，启发学生思考爱好和职业间的因果关系，学生的回答可用“He like sports, so he can be a coach.”等句型。

3. 写作准备环节。

学生根据在阅读中找到的因果关系，思考自己的兴趣爱好和对应的职业，完成自己的职业规划指南。

教师引导学生思考，在实际生活中，个人爱好不止一项，想要做的工作也不止一种，但除了兴趣外，还有其他现实因素需要考虑，比如工作的地点可能离家太远，或者工作会非常忙而没有业余时间等，让学生在综合考虑过后再写下最终选择。

4. 表达与分享环节。

学生根据写作提示完成写作练习，并与同伴分享。

思维试纸：

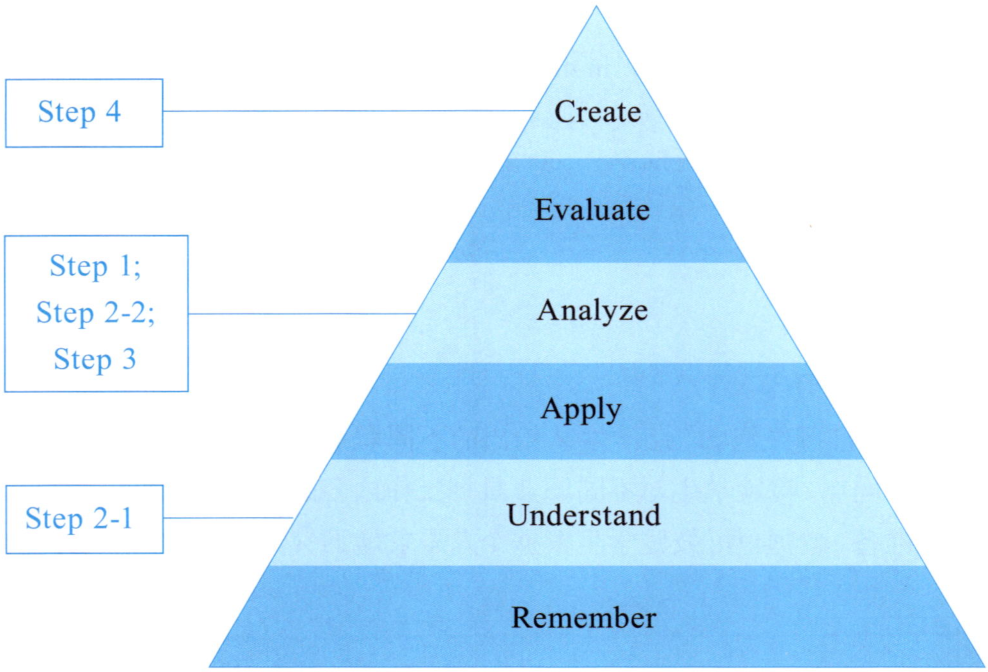

Part Three Vocabulary

教学素材: businessman (businesswoman), pilot, fisherman (fisherwoman), taxi driver, factory worker, postman, police officer, scientist, coach, cleaner, writer, singer, dancer, football player

教学步骤:

Step 1 Guessing

Who are these people in the following pictures? Try to **guess** their jobs and write them down.

(1) __________

(2) __________

(3) __________

(4) __________

(5) __________

Step 2 Multiple Choice

Pick up one word from each group, and the word you choose should be different from the other two words. You should explain your choice to your partner.

(　　) (1)	A. postman	B. coach	C. writer
(　　) (2)	A. fisherman	B. football player	C. taxi driver
(　　) (3)	A. office	B. university	C. pilot
(　　) (4)	A. dangerous	B. healthy	C. great
(　　) (5)	A. bus	B. gym	C. bike

教学时长: 15 mins

教学建议:

1. 词汇部分主要用于练习，旨在巩固词汇和语法知识。

2. 学生自行在课前或课后完成，教师批改或让学生在课堂上分享展示，及时纠错。

3. "Step 1" 中学生需在横线上写出图中名人所从事的工作，如果不认识，也可以根据图中线索进行猜测；"Step 2" 中学生需要通过分析找出每一组中和其他两个单词不同的单词，并和同伴解释这样分类的原因，这道练习有一定开放性，如第1题和第2题无标准答案，学生言之成理即可，可以参考的答案和理由如下：

(1) C　"Postman" and "coach" need to run outside, but "writer" can work at home.

(2) A　"Fisherman" needs to work near water, but "football player" and "taxi driver" should work on the ground.

(3) C　"Office" and "university" are work places, but "pilot" is a job.

(4) A　"Healthy" and "great" are positive words, but "dangerous" has negative meaning.

(5) B　"Bus" and "bike" are means of transportation, but "gym" is a work place.

思维试纸:

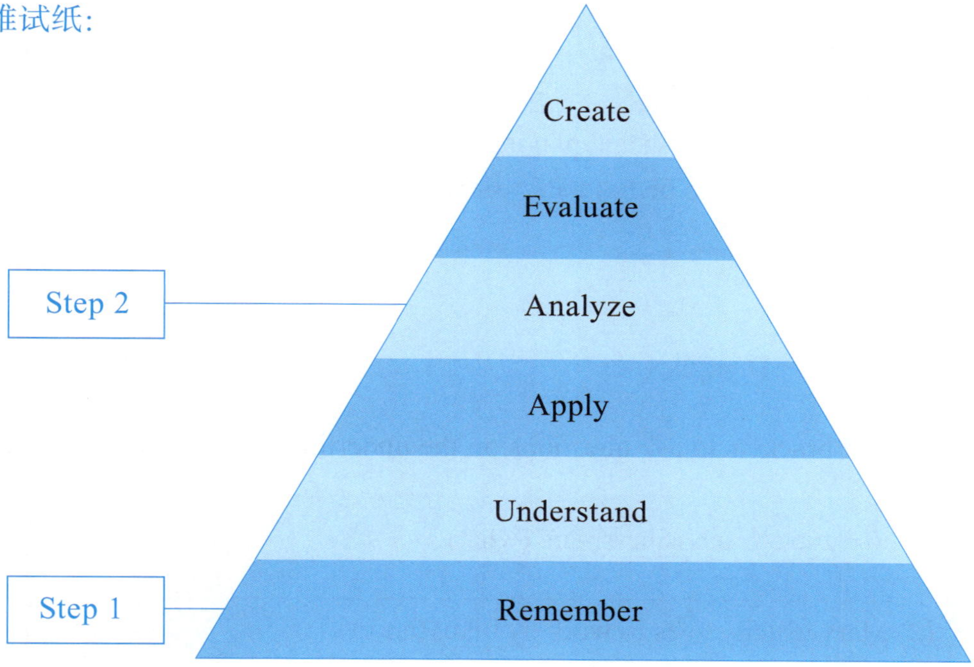

Part Four Grammar

教学素材: What does… do?

Where does he/she work?

How does he/she go to work?

教学步骤:

Step 1 Self-checking

Choose the right word in brackets to complete the following sentences.

(1) —________ (How/Where/What) does he do?

—He is a factory worker.

(2) —________ (How/Where/What) does Miss Yang go to work?

—She works in an office nearby, so she goes to work on foot.

(3) — ______ (How/Where/What) do Jim and John work?

— They work in a gym.

(4) Wu Yifan is good at ________ (use/uses/using) computers.

(5) Sarah likes running and playing ping-pong, and she wants ________ (to/to be/be) a PE teacher.

Step 2 Further Practicing

Use the word in brackets to ask questions on the underlined part in each sentence.

(1) My uncle is a <u>businessman</u>. (what)

____

(2) Mary usually goes to work <u>by bike</u>. (how)

____

(3) Jim likes science and he works <u>in a university</u>. (where)

____

(4) John and Mike are colleagues and they often go to work together <u>by car</u>. (how)

____

(5) My sister likes <u>sports</u> and she wants to be a coach. (what)

____

教学时长: 15 mins

教学建议:

1. 语法部分旨在巩固学生对重点句型的运用。本单元要求学生掌握运用“what”“how”“where”引导的特殊疑问句询问工作信息。

2. 学生可自行在课前或课后完成，教师批改或让学生互相批改，及时纠错。

3. “Step 1” 中学生需从括号中选出正确的单词完成句子，“Step 2” 中学生需使用括号中的词对句子画线部分提问，均考查学生对相应问句及回答中易错点的掌握情况。

思维试纸：

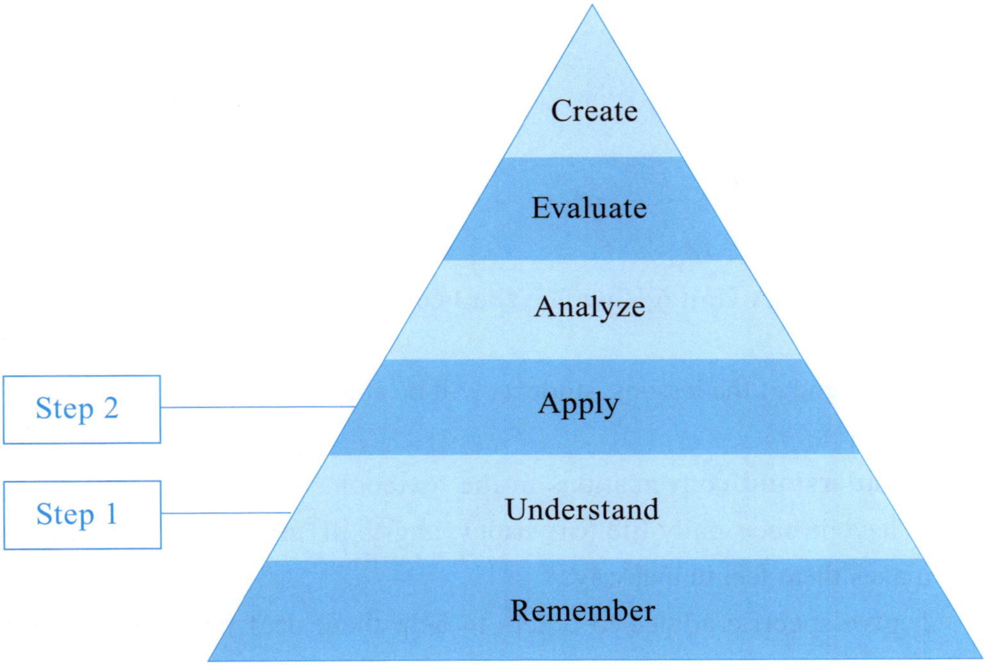

Unit 6　How Do You Feel?

单元导览

单元话题: 情感与情绪
素材来源: PEP 6A Unit 6 How Do You Feel?
教学目标:

By the end of the lessons, students will be able to

语言目标:

1. **understand** conversations in the textbook, **talk about** feelings they usually have in their daily life (e.g. happy, angry, ill, afraid, sad, worried) and what makes them feel in that way;

2. **give** specific advice to others to help them deal with their negative feelings;

3. **observe** the changes of a process, and **record** the change of their own feelings within a day by using flow map;

4. **comprehend** the meaning of the story, **analyze** the main content and structure, and **apply** the knowledge and language in the story to writing about their own ideas in another situation.

非语言目标:

1. develop empathy for other people's situation;

2. work in groups and collaborate with others to finish tasks related to their daily life about places and directions;

3. strengthen their higher order thinking skills: **analyzing** and **creating**;

4. **make** conversations in given situations with creative thinking and **judge** with critical thinking.

融思设计

Part One Listening and Speaking

教学素材: Part B Let's Talk
教学步骤:

Step 1 Preparation before Listening

Look at the picture in the textbook and **guess**: Do they go to the zoo?

If yes, how do they feel? If not, why don't they go?

____

____

____

Step 2 Listening Comprehension

Listen and **choose** the right answers.

(1) Why don't they go to the zoo?

A. Because the weather is bad.

B. Because Sam's dad is ill.

C. Because the zoo is closed today.

(2) Where do the go at last?

A. They go to school.

B. They go back home.

C. They go to the hospital.

Step 3 Preparation before Speaking

Look at the these pictures, imagine you are in different situations and **think about** how you feel.

e.g. a sunny day	a snowy day
in a dark night	take an exam
visit a zoo	have a Chinese/math/English… class

Step 4 Speaking and Sharing

1. Choose a picture with your group member, write down your feelings in this situation and **make** a magic carpet for your group. You need to write down feelings first, and ask the reasons of each other's feelings.

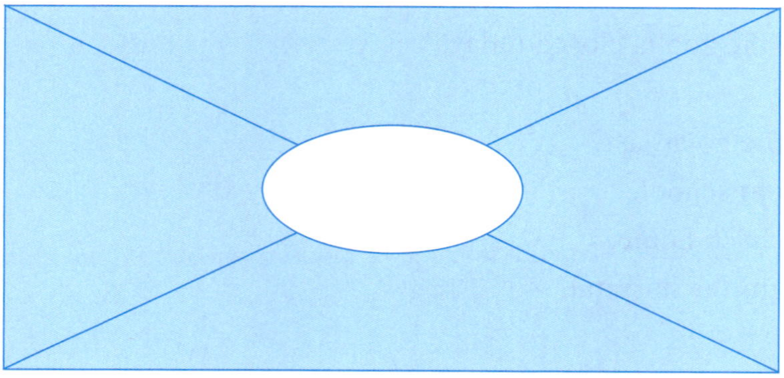

First, write down feelings in groups.

This is an example of a magic carpet.

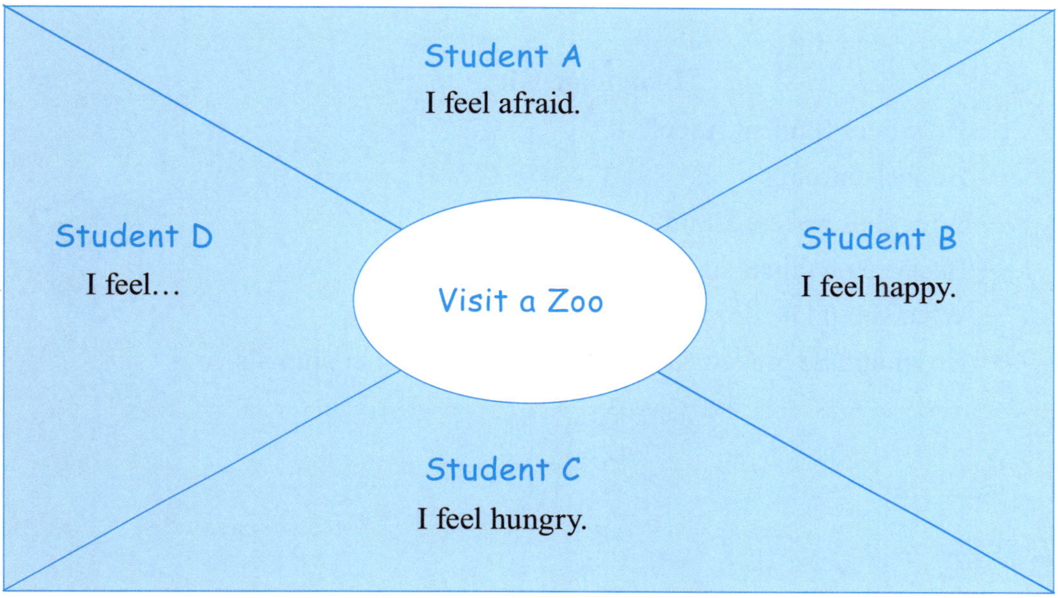

Then, ask the reason of each feeling and write it down.

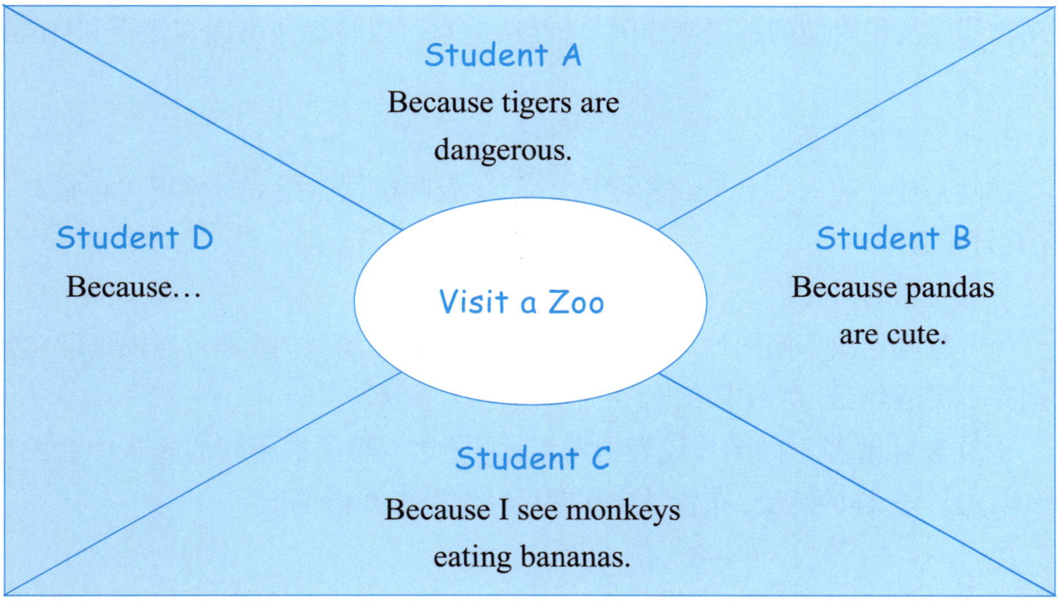

2. Based on your magic carpet, make a conversation with your group members to **talk about** the feelings. You can also ask for advice if you think he/she needs help.

Language Kit

— How does Student A feel?

— He feels afraid.

— Why does he feel afraid?

— Because he thinks tigers are dangerous.

— What should he do?

— He should be brave/take a deep breath/visit other animals...

教学时长: 1 hr

教学建议:

1. 听前准备环节。

教师让学生根据配图预测对话涉及的内容，训练学生在听前结合已有信息和生活经验来预测听力内容的能力。教师可以让学生先根据配图猜测图中人物是否去动物园以及相对应的感受和原因。学生听完后可以验证所听内容是否和自己的预测一致。

2. 听力理解环节。

教师播放一遍对话音频，学生完成练习。教师根据学生完成情况可再播放一遍，并订正答案。

3. 表达准备环节。

(1) 教师给出不同图片，每种图片代表一个常见场景。教师可以根据课堂需求选择不同的场景，练习中给出了六个场景作为参考。

(2) 教师解释不同图片代表的场景，引导学生想象在不同的场景中会发生什么事，会有怎样的感受，布置学生在课后仔细思考并做笔记。

4. 表达与分享环节。

（1）学生以小组为单位选择一个共同感兴趣的场景，询问组员在不同场景中可能经历的事件及感受，完成“magic carpet”，需注意事件和感受之间的因果联系，运用情绪相关单词和句型“I feel...”。

（2）学生在完成“magic carpet”时，可以先观察示例。该工具便于记录不同学生对同一个话题的发言内容，可以直观地呈现本组同学的讨论结果。

（3）完成本组的“magic carpet”后，学生可参考课文内容和“Language Kit”编对话，在询问感受后给出相应建议，练习“How do you/does he feel?”“What should I/he do?”“You/He should...”等句型。

（4）教师引导学生理解在同样的情景下，不同的人会有不同的感受。每个人的感受都有合理性，学生应该学会意识到自己真实的感受，也可以根据不同的情绪给他人相应的建议。

思维试纸：

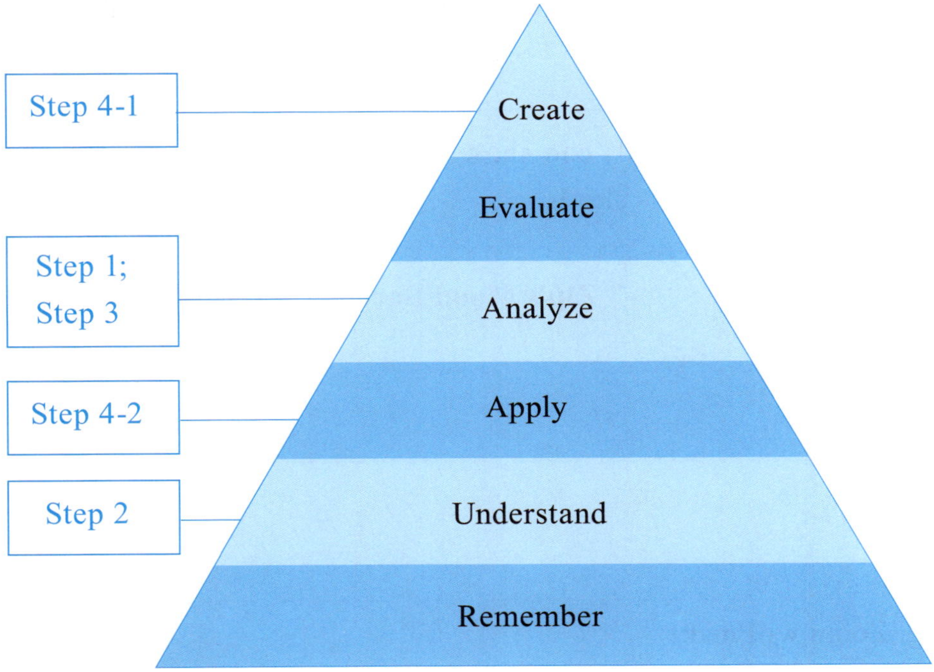

Part Two　Reading and Writing

教学素材: Part B　Read and Write
教学步骤:

Step 1　Preparation before Reading

Observe Zip's facial expressions in Pictures 2, 4 and 6 in the textbook. Do you **find** any differences? Share your findings with your partner.

Picture 2	→	Picture 4	→	Picture 6
Zip is ________.		Zip is ________.		Zip is ________.

Step 2　Reading Comprehension

Read the story, and **finish** the following flow map.
You need to find the changes of Zip's feelings, and the causes to make her feelings change.

A flow map (流程图) can show steps/changes in a process clearly.

Zip's Mood Barometer (晴雨表)

e.g. happy →	→	
↑	↑	↑
e.g. Zoom will make some popcorn.		

Step 3 Preparation before Writing

After finishing Zip's mood barometer, you can try to make your own mood barometer.

My Mood Barometer

e.g. worried →	→	
↑	↑	↑
e.g. In the morning, I'm late for school.	e.g. In the afternoon, ________________.	e.g. At night, ______ ________________.

Step 4 Writing and Sharing

Share your mood barometer with your partner and **finish** the following writing.

> I have different feelings within a day. In the morning, I am ________ because ________________________. Then, in the afternoon, ____, so I feel ________________. At night, I feel ________ because ____.

教学时长: 1 hr

教学建议:

1. 读前准备环节。

(1) 教师让学生根据文章配图预测文章可能讲述的内容，训练学生预测文本的能力；此处选择了文章中 "Zip" 情绪有明显变化的几张图，学生需要仔细观察并猜测这几张图中 "Zip" 到底是什么心情，教师可以进一步引导学生思考

"Zip" 的心情产生了什么变化，可能是由什么原因引起的。

（2）流程图（flow map）的引入旨在呈现过程中每个环节的具体内容。学生可以直观地看到完整的过程和过程中产生的变化。

2. 阅读理解环节。

学生读完短文后，教师引导学生根据对文章的理解完成图表，检查学生对文章逻辑和细节的理解。学生填入"Zip" 确切的心情变化和导致心情变化的具体事件，教师可以引导学生和读前环节的流程图进行对比，让学生检查自己的预测是否准确。

3. 写作准备环节。

（1）教师引导学生以 "Zip" 情绪的变化为线索复述故事，总结情绪会在不同的时间和事件下产生变化。

（2）教师带领学生回忆他们一天的心情，比如上午、下午、晚上的心情分别是怎样的，让学生思考一天中自己的情绪波动，为课后完成制作 "我的心情晴雨表" 做准备。

4. 表达与分享环节。

同伴互相分享交流自己的心情晴雨表，并根据写作提示完成写作练习。

思维试纸：

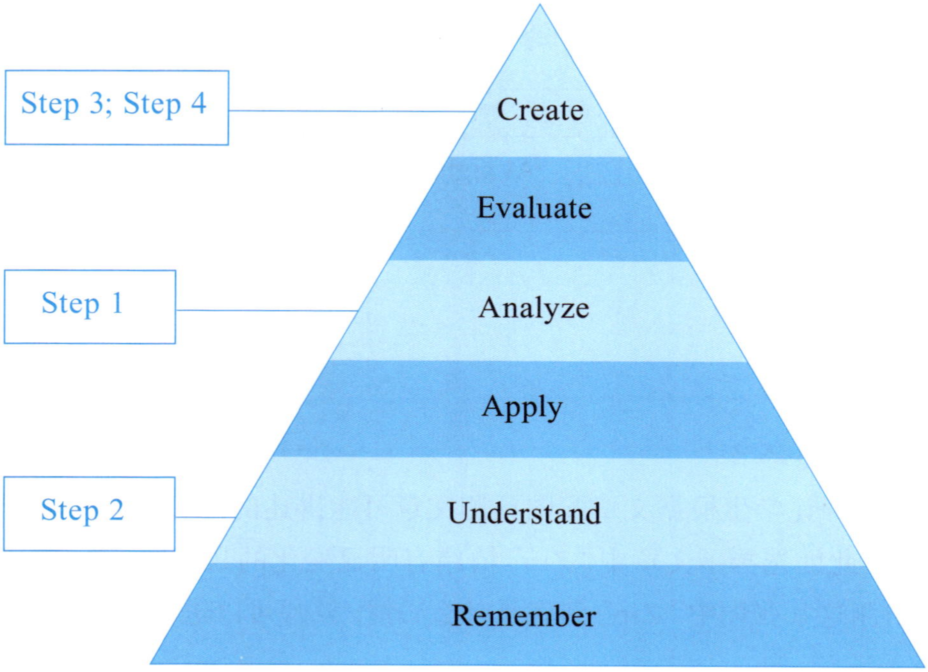

Part Three Vocabulary

教学素材: happy, angry, ill, afraid, sad, worried

教学步骤:

Step 1 Guessing

Look at the following famous paintings and **guess** what feelings they represent. You can also discuss with your **partner** about what makes people in the paintings have such feelings.

(1) ____________

(2) ____________

(3) ____________

Step 2 Defining

Do you have your own understanding of different feelings? Please try to use your own way to **define** different feelings.

"Define" means you need to use your own words to explain something to others.
You can't see or touch feelings, but you can try to use words to help others see or touch them.

e.g.
Happy is a red balloon.
Sad is a raining night.

(1) Sad is ______________________________.
(2) Worried is ______________________________.
(3) Happy is ______________________________.
(4) Angry is ______________________________.
(5) Afraid is ______________________________.
(6) Ill is ______________________________.

教学时长: 15 mins

教学建议:

1. 词汇部分主要用于练习，旨在巩固词汇和语法知识。

2. 学生自行在课前或课后完成，教师批改或让学生在课堂上分享展示，及时纠错。

3. 课堂上，教师带领学生总结存在的问题和解决办法，注重引导学生巩固对本单元重点单词词性、词义的理解。

4. "Step 1" 中学生需根据自己的理解猜测并写下名画中人物的情绪，完成后可以和同伴讨论人物产生该情绪可能的原因，答案并不唯一，言之成理即可。

5. "Step 2" 中学生需根据对本单元所学情绪相关词汇的理解，用自己的语言对不同的情绪下定义，既考查了学生的理解和表达能力，又充分锻炼了学生的想象力和创造力；在练习解释抽象事物时，教师可以引导学生尝试用形容词加非抽象名词的方式进行解释，并在全班分享交流，选出学生们最喜欢的情绪定义。

思维试纸:

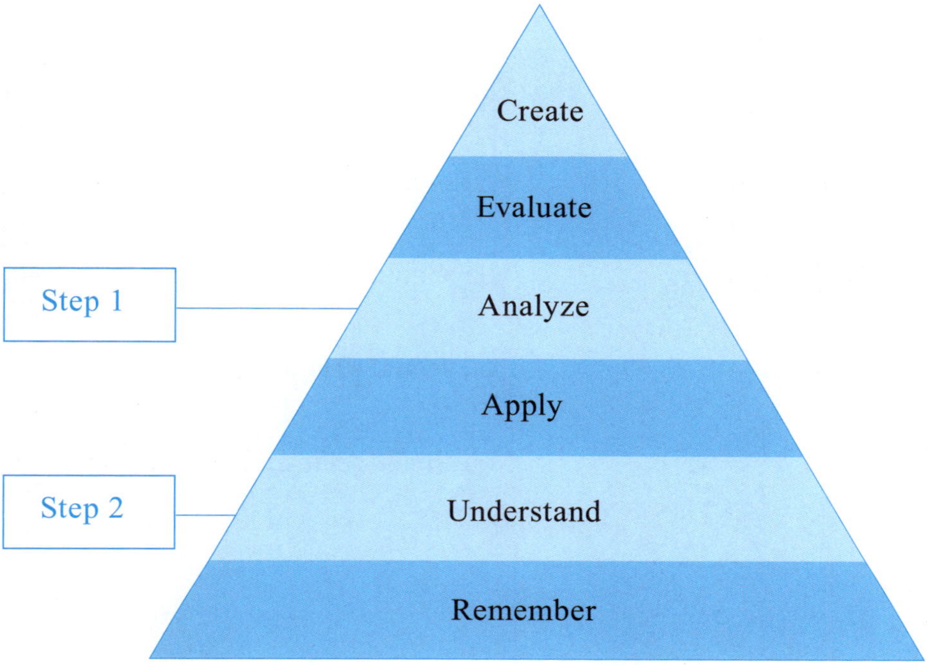

Part Four Grammar

教学素材: — How do you feel?
— I feel.../I am...

— How does he/she feel?
— He/She feels...

— What should I do?
— You should...

教学步骤:

Step 1 Self-checking

Match and discuss with your partner to give more suggestions to each feeling.

What should I do?

I feel angry.	You should turn on the light at night.
I feel ill.	You should take a deep breath.
I feel worried.	You should see a doctor.
I feel afraid.	You should read a joke.
I feel sad.	You should relax and enjoy a movie.

Step 2 Further Practicing

Based on the given answers, **write down** proper questions.

(1) ____________________________?	I feel worried.
(2) ____________________________?	She should see a doctor.
(3) ____________________________?	He is angry.
(4) ____________________________?	I'm making popcorn.

教学时长: 15 mins

教学建议:

1. 语法部分旨在巩固学生对重点句型的运用。本单元要求学生运用相关句型询问情绪和给出建议。

2. 学生可自行在课前或课后完成，教师批改或让学生互相批改，及时纠错。

3. “Step 1”中学生需将情绪和对应的可行建议连线搭配，巩固对相关句型的理解与应用；“Step 2”中学生需根据给出的回答写出对应的问题，练习使用“how”和“what”引导的特殊疑问句，并注意动词的第三人称单数。

思维试纸：

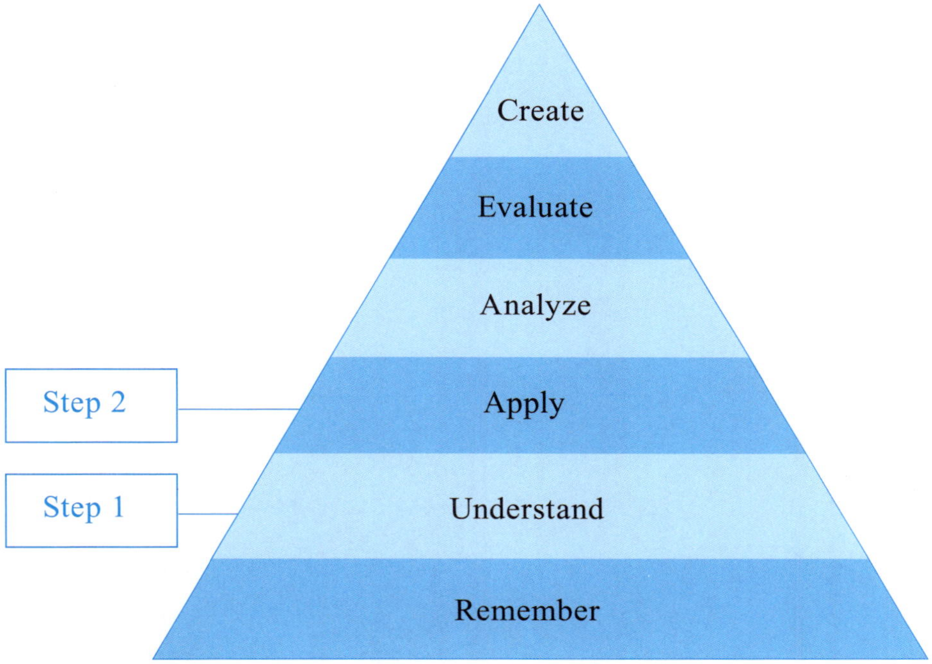

6B

Unit 1 How Tall Are You?

单元导览

单元话题: 个人信息

素材来源: PEP 6B Unit 1 How Tall Are You?

教学目标:

By the end of the lesson, students will be able to

语言目标:

1. **compare** certain features of objects/persons by **using** the comparative degree of adjectives/adverbs and the sentence pattern: … is/are ~er than…;

2. **understand** the conversations in the textbook, **choose** their favorite schoolbags by **comparing** the given schoolbags and offer reasons **using** the sentence patterns: … is/are ~er than…; I would like…; … because…;

3. **comprehend** the meaning of the story, **analyze** the main content, and write about their pleasant changes by using the comparative degree of adjectives/adverbs;

4. **understand** the superlative degree of adjectives/adverbs and put the objects/persons into the correct **order** from the highest degree to the lowest degree;

5. **deduce** the rules for the comparative/superlative degree of adjectives/adverbs and **change** the given adjectives/adverbs into their corresponding comparative/superlative degree.

非语言目标:

1. **associate** physical knowledge about the production of shadow;

2. **realize** their own progress and have a positive attitude towards their own growth and future;

3. work in groups to finish tasks and to learn from others;

4. **strengthen** their higher order thinking skills: **analyzing**, **evaluating** and **creating**;

5. **compare** and **judge** with problem-solving and decision-making skills.

融思设计

Part One Listening and Speaking

教学素材: Part B Let's Talk

教学步骤:

Step 1 Listening Comprehension

Mike and Wu Yifan are among the following eight children. **Find** them **out** with the clues in the recording.

1. Listen and find Mike and Wu Yifan. **Complete** the sentences below first.

Wu Yifan's shoes are size ________.
Mike's shoes are size ________.

Then, **mark** all the kids who might be Mike with "M", and Wu with "W".

2. Listen again and **find out** the taller one between Mike and Wu Yifan. Tick him first.

Mike/Wu Yifan is taller.

Cross out all the kids who can't be Mike or Wu Yifan.

3. Listen to the dialogue for the third time. Who is heavier, Mike or Wu Yifan? **Complete** the sentence below first.

Wu Yifan is ________ kilograms and Mike is ________ kilograms.

Do you know who is Mike and who is Wu Yifan now? **Circle** them **out**.

4. **Fill in** the blanks with what you know about Mike and Wu Yifan.

Mike is ________ than Wu Yifan.
Wu Yifan is ________ than Mike.
Mike wears ________ shoes than Wu Yifan does.

Step 2 Preparation before Speaking

1. If your schoolbag is broken and you want to buy a new one, there are two schoolbags you may choose from. Can you **compare** them and write down some sentences by using "than" in the table below? You can add more features.

Schoolbag A

Schoolbag B

价格:	¥ 99
面料:	帆布
尺寸:	42 cm×30 cm×18 cm
重量:	0.65 kg
内袋数量:	4
肩带:	加厚减负肩带

价格:	¥ 125
面料:	尼龙+皮革
尺寸:	38 cm×28 cm×16 cm
重量:	0.80 kg
内袋数量:	6
肩带:	减负肩带

Features	**Differences**
Price	Schoolbag A is ______________ than Schoolbag B.
Size	Schoolbag A is ______________ than Schoolbag B.
Weight	Schoolbag A is ______________ than Schoolbag B.
No. of Bags	Schoolbag B has ______________ than Schoolbag A.

2. When you choose a schoolbag, which features above will help you to make a decision? **Write down** three ones from the most important to the least.

Most Important → Less Important

Step 3 Speaking and Sharing

1. Each student **decides** on his/her favorite schoolbag and **offers** at least three reasons.

I would like ____________.

Because ________________.

2. Share your preference and the reasons with group members. **Find** all the partners who have the same choice as you and **summarize** your reasons below.

__________________ of my group members have the same choice as me.

The reasons are:

(1) ____

____

(2) ____

____

(3) ____

____

教学时长: 1.5 hrs

教学建议:

1. 听力理解环节。

(1)本活动进行过程中要求按照三个线索的顺序进行识别和筛除;教师可根据学生对听力材料的理解程度来决定是否需要播放第三遍录音。

(2)如果只播放两遍录音即可,那么播放第二遍录音后,学生按顺序完成第2、3项活动。

(3)第4项为总结活动。教师可以根据学生的理解情况和口语表达能力灵活处理活动难度,可以要求学生只完成填空,也可鼓励学生利用填空后的语句口头陈述。

参考答案:

37, 40; Wu Yifan; 46, 48; heavier, taller, bigger

2. 表达准备环节。

(1)学生在课堂上通过教师引导完成各项活动。

（2）活动1：填写表格时，教师可根据学生需要，辅助其完成比较书包特征的句子："I like blue better." "There are more bags in Schoolbag B." "Schoolbag A is cheaper than Schoolbag B." "Schoolbag A is more comfortable (beautiful/durable/fashionable/cheaper) than Schoolbag B." 教师应鼓励学生做更多的比较，填在表格中。

（3）活动2：教师应注意引导学生提炼和总结方法，帮助学生明白应该如何做选择，而不是仅局限于这两个书包的选择。

3. 表达与分享环节。

（1）活动1：教师让学生先自己利用句子结构准备语言。教师应提醒学生尽量使用"Step 2"中表格里描述差异的句子，也可以从个人的喜好来说明。

（2）活动2：学生在组内介绍自己的选择，要求学生一定要说出至少三个理由。教师可根据学生情况，将该活动延展为：每组推选两个不同选择的同学将本组相同选择的同学的意见汇报给全班同学。教师注意引导学生使用目标语言（例如：We/I think Schoolbag A is... than Schoolbag B.）。同时，教师也可以鼓励学生使用曾经学过的语言来陈述理由（例如：Pink is my favorite color.）。

思维试纸：

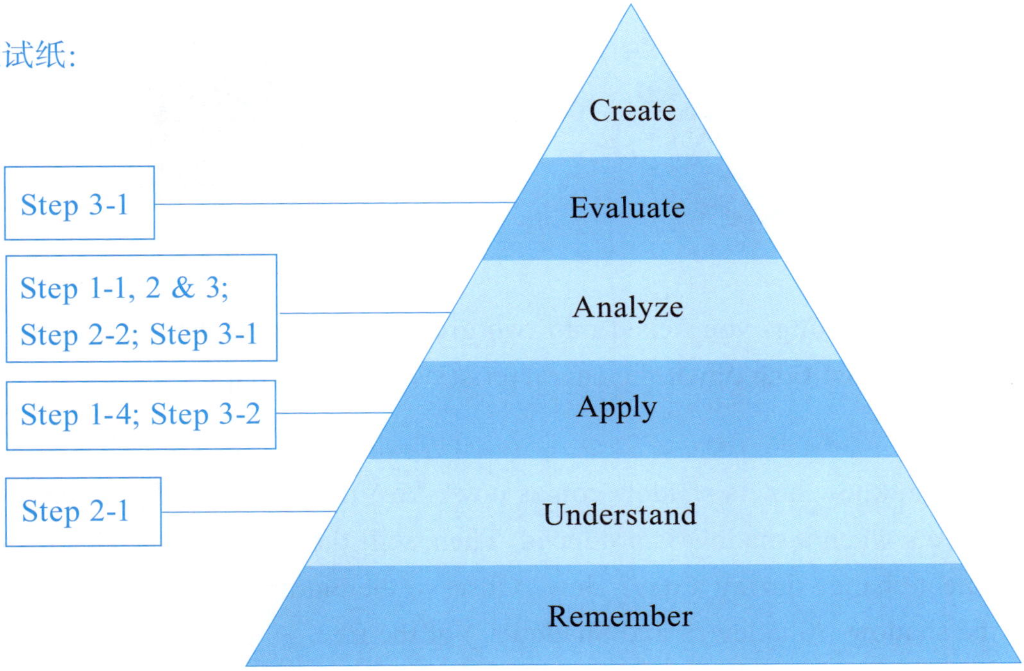

备注："思维试纸"将各教学活动中加粗的动词（思维技能）与思维层级匹配，使教学过程中的思维技能训练显性化。6B余下各单元的"思维试纸"不再一一备注。

Part Two　Reading and Writing

教学素材: Part B　Read and Write

教学步骤:

Step 1　Preparation before Reading

1. Do you know how a shadow comes? **Tick** the things which can help to produce a shadow.

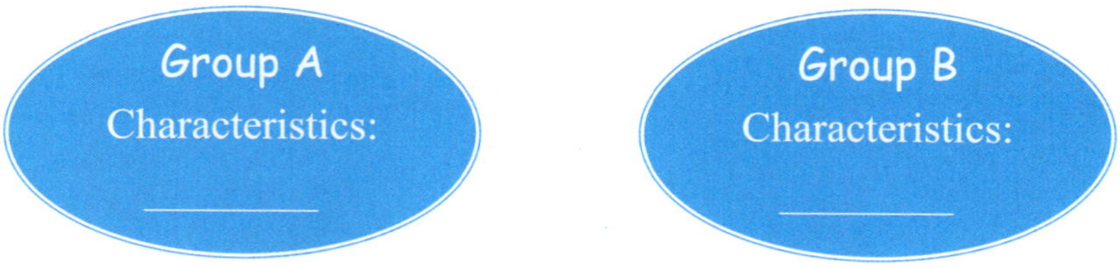

2. Put all the things you ticked into two groups and **match** the pictures with the circles. Then **take down** the characteristics of each group.

3. Do you know how a shadow comes now? Yes, there must be light and opaque objects when a shadow is produced. Then, will the length of the shadow of an object change during a day? How? Observe the picture below and try to **draw** the shadows (Shadow B and Shadow C) of the tree.

4. Order the three shadows from the longest with "1" to the shortest with "3".

Shadow A	Shadow B	Shadow C

Step 2 Reading Comprehension

1. Read and **answer** these questions.

(1) What is Little Duck doing?

He is ________ the sun goes down.

(2) What does Little Duck notice?

His shadow is getting ________ (longer/shorter) when the sun goes lower.

(3) What does Little Duck ask?

Why is his shadow ________ when the sun gets ________?

(4) How does Old Tree answer?

He says that because Little Duck gets ________ so his shadow gets ________ when the sun goes lower.

2. Group work.

(1) Do you agree with Old Tree? **Observe** the picture below and then **draw** the shadows of Little Duck when he gets taller.

Compare the shadows in the picture. Are they getting longer and longer? Is Old Tree right?

(2) **Work out** an answer to Little Duck's question. You may consult the picture in Task 3 of Step 1, your science teacher or the Internet.

Step 3　Writing and Sharing

1. Do you still remember how you looked like when you were in Grade One? Find a picture of you at that time and paste it below.

2. There are a lot of changes happened to you. Please **write down** at least eight sentences talking about some of these changes. You may **use** sentence structures below while writing.

Tip: I am…
I can…
My… is…
I have…

	Changes	Results

3. Among all these changes, what are good and what are not so good? **Tick** the good changes in the first column of the above table.

4. Good changes always bring good results, say, when you grow taller, you can see further away. **Work out** some results of these good changes and take them down in Column 3 in the above table.

5. Now you are ready to **write** an essay about your pleasant changes. Follow your teacher and take down the sentences here. You will get a wonderful essay.

My Pleasant Changes

My name is __________. This is a photo of mine when I was six. Now, I'm ______________________________________（现在的年龄）

____

____

____

____

____

____（所有好变化和好结果）

It's ________________ to get older. I like what I am!

教学时长：1 hr

教学建议：

1. 读前准备环节。

（1）教师引导学生调取自身储备的有关知识，回想影子产生的原理及要素。

（2）教师提示学生将所给物品分成两类并提炼各自性质：光源和不透明物体。学生不必使用英文表达。教师应特别提醒学生将提炼的性质填写在上一题图示中的圆圈里。

（3）教师引导学生根据太阳在位置A时的阴影，画出太阳在位置B和C时的阴影，要求学生分别命名三个阴影区域为"Shadow A""Shadow B"和"Shadow C"。

（4）学生比较三个阴影的长度并排序，从最长到最短分别为：3，2，1。

2. 阅读理解环节。

（1）回答问题：学生根据短文内容填空。

参考答案：

watching; longer; longer; lower; taller/older; longer

（2）小组活动。

画阴影：教师引导学生用笔和尺子把小鸭子长高后的阴影画出来，并让学生观察，随着身体长高，影子是不是"长"长了。学生在组内讨论并自由评价大树给出的答案。学生可用中文回答。

找答案：学生课后分组完成。教师鼓励学生通过不同的渠道和方式求证答案，并能够将其中的科学原理清楚地讲出来。学生可用中文或英文回答。下节课时可作为课前热身和复习，教师在每组请一位代表来介绍本组的发现。

3. 写作与分享环节。

（1）教师课前请每位学生将一张自己一年级时的全身照贴在相应位置。

（2）教师引导学生通过比较今昔尽可能多地发现发生在自己身上的变化，并使用“can”“am”“have”“is”等动词引导形容词或副词比较级来描述自己的变化，如：“I have more friends.”“I can run faster.”“I am taller.”“My hair is longer.”每位同学至少要写出8句话。

（3）教师让学生从已有的变化中勾选出好的、积极的变化并使用“I can...”或者比较级句式来说明积极变化带来的好的结果。学生只需选择其中能够说明好的结果的来写，不必每条都写。

（4）写作时，教师首先让学生把自己的信息填进相关空格中，并写下自己的年纪；然后让学生把在第2题表格中的描述好的变化和结果的句子一一写进作文里；最后，引导学生得出“长大真好”的结论，并在倒数第二句话中填上“good”。作文就写好了。

思维试纸：

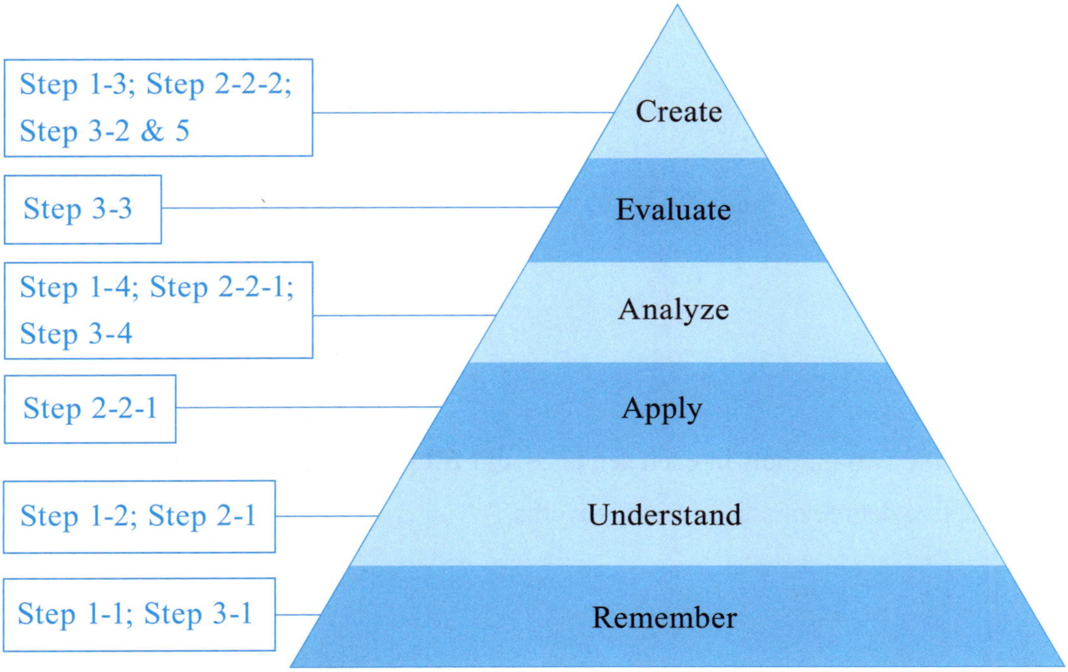

Part Three　Vocabulary

教学素材: younger, older, taller, shorter, longer, thinner, heavier, bigger, smaller, fatter, stronger, dinosaur, hall, meter, than, both, kilogram, countryside, lower, shadow, smarter

教学步骤:

Step 1　Word-making

Make words with the letters below. Each letter can be used more than once. Write as many words as you can and share your work with your partner.

Step 2　Comparing and Blank-filling

Compare the two animals in each sentence and **fill in** the blanks with the comparative or superlative degree of adjectives or adverbs.

(1) A bird flies __________ than a cock.
(2) A giraffe is __________ than a horse.
(3) A rabbit is __________ than a bear.
(4) A pig is __________ than a goat.
(5) A mouse runs __________ than a caterpillar.
(6) Human beings are __________ than monkeys.
(7) The whale is the __________ animal in the sea.
(8) The elephant has the __________ nose on the earth.

教学时长: 30 mins

教学建议:

1. 词汇部分主要用于练习，旨在巩固词汇和语法知识。

2. 学生自行在课前或课后完成。课堂上，学生展示和分享作业，教师纠错。

3. "Step 1"为开放式问题，学生可以任意拼写出自己知道的单词，教师可以要求学生写出单词的中文意思，也可以组织全班比赛，看谁写出的正确单词最多。

4. "Step 2"中多个小题不止一个答案，教师可以鼓励学生开动脑筋找出动物的差别。

参考答案:

(1) higher
(2) taller/heavier/bigger
(3) smaller/lighter
(4) fatter/bigger
(5) faster
(6) smarter/bigger/stronger
(7) biggest
(8) longest

思维试纸:

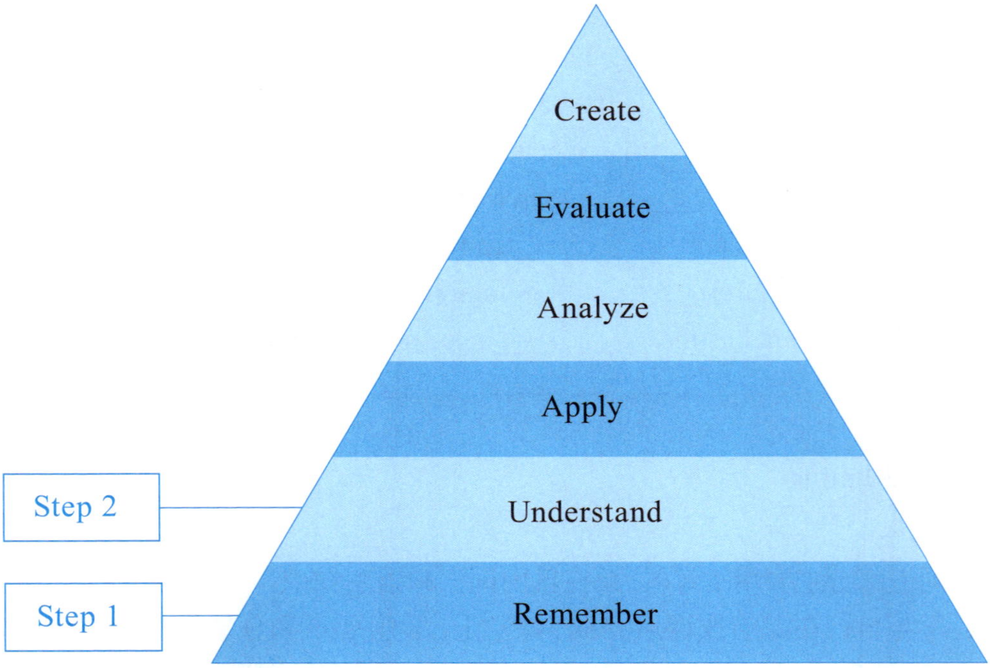

Part Four Grammar

教学素材: 1. The comparative degree and superlative degree of adjectives or adverbs;
2. Sentence pattern: ... ~er than...

教学步骤:

Step 1 Self-checking

Link the adjective or adverb with its comparative degree and its superlative degree.

形容词或副词	比较级	最高级
tall	earlier	fattest
big	longer	thinnest
thin	heavier	tallest
short	bigger	shortest
fast	fatter	longest
heavy	shorter	fastest
fat	taller	biggest
long	faster	heaviest
early	thinner	earliest

Step 2 Rule-finding

1. **Circle** what shares in the comparative degree and superlative degree in the above adjectives or adverbs.

2. **Summarize** how to make the comparative degree and superlative degree of the adjectives or adverbs.

Step 3 Further Practicing

1. **Write down** the comparative degree and the superlative degree of the following words.

	比较级	最高级
young	________	________
strong	________	________
happy	________	________

2. **Order** the boys in each groups from the highest degree ("1") to the lowest degree ("3") according to the given descriptions.

(1) Boy B is heavier than Boy A. Boy C is the heaviest among them.

Boy A ☐ Boy B ☐ Boy C ☐

(2) Boy C's hair is long. Boy A's hair is longer than Boy C's. Boy B's hair is longer than Boy A's.

Boy A ☐ Boy B ☐ Boy C ☐

(3) Boy A runs very fast. But he runs slower than Boy C. Boy B runs faster than Boy C.

Boy A ☐ Boy B ☐ Boy C ☐

(4) Boy B gets up early every morning. But Boy A and C get up even earlier than Boy B. Boy A gets up the earliest every morning.

Boy A ☐ Boy B ☐ Boy C ☐

(5) Boy A is the oldest. Boy B is older than Boy C.

Boy A ☐ Boy B ☐ Boy C ☐

教学时长: 30 mins

教学建议:

1. 语法部分主要用于练习,旨在巩固词汇和语法知识。本单元要求学生掌握运用形容词/副词的比较级和最高级。

2. 学生自行在课前或课后完成,教师批改。

3. 课堂上,教师带领学生总结存在的问题和解决办法。

思维试纸:

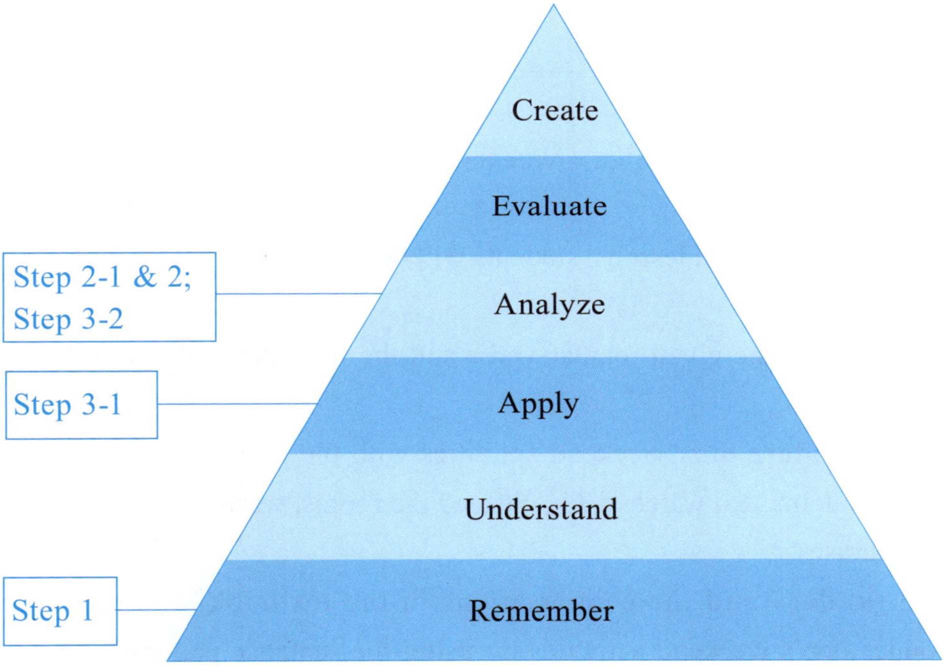

Unit 2 Last Weekend

单元导览

单元话题: 周末活动

素材来源: PEP 6B Unit 2 Last Weekend

教学目标:

By the end of the lessons, students will be able to

语言目标:

1. **change** the given regular verbs and the irregular verbs into their past forms;

2. **introduce** their weekend activities with the past form of such verbal phrases as drank tea, watched TV, cleaned the rooms, washed clothes and other verbal phrases;

3. **understand** the conversations in the textbook, and ask for and introduce one's weekend activities by **using** the sentence patterns: "How was your weekend?" "What did you do last weekend?" "What else did you do?" "It was good/bad/not bad/so so/boring/tiring/tedious";

4. **comprehend** the meaning of the complaint letter, know how to make a general comment on an experience and **support** it with facts in speaking and writing, and write about their weekend activities with past tense;

5. **know** the differences between present tense and past tense in terms of usage and forms and **use** both tenses correctly to state what happened and what exists.

非语言目标:

1. learn to listen to others carefully and give reasons to **persuade** others;

2. work in groups to finish tasks and to learn from others;

3. develop their divergent **thinking**;

4. strengthen their higher order thinking skills: **analyzing**, **evaluating** and **creating**;

5. **compare** and **judge** with evaluating and decision-making skills.

融思设计

Part One Listening and Speaking

教学素材: Part A Let's Talk

教学步骤:

Step 1 Listening Comprehension

1. **Match** the pictures to the acts.

drank tea | watched TV | cleaned the rooms | washed clothes

Mike

Mike's grandpa

2. Listen and try your best to **finish** the following exercises.

(1) Who stayed at home last weekend, Mike or his grandpa? Tick the right answer.

☐ Mike ☐ Mike's grandpa

(2) **Match** the above acts with Mike or his grandpa according to what you hear from the dialogue.

3. Listen to the dialogue again. Try your best to do the following exercises.

(1) Did you hear how Mike and his grandpa asked about their weekend? Complete the sentences below with what you hear from the dialogue.

(2) How did Mike and his grandpa think of their weekend? Take down the sentences they said to comment on their weekend.

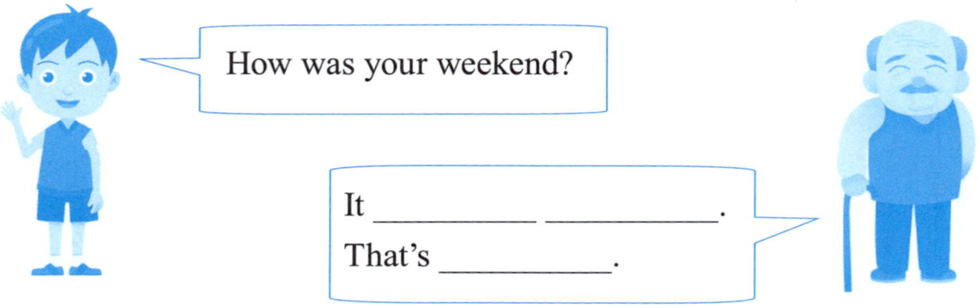

Step 2 Preparation before Speaking

1. What do you usually do at the weekend? Generally, you have two options, to stay at home or to go out. Discuss in groups and work out as many verbs as you can to describe what you can do at the weekend. **Only verbs!** Then **take down** the past forms of the verbs in the circles.

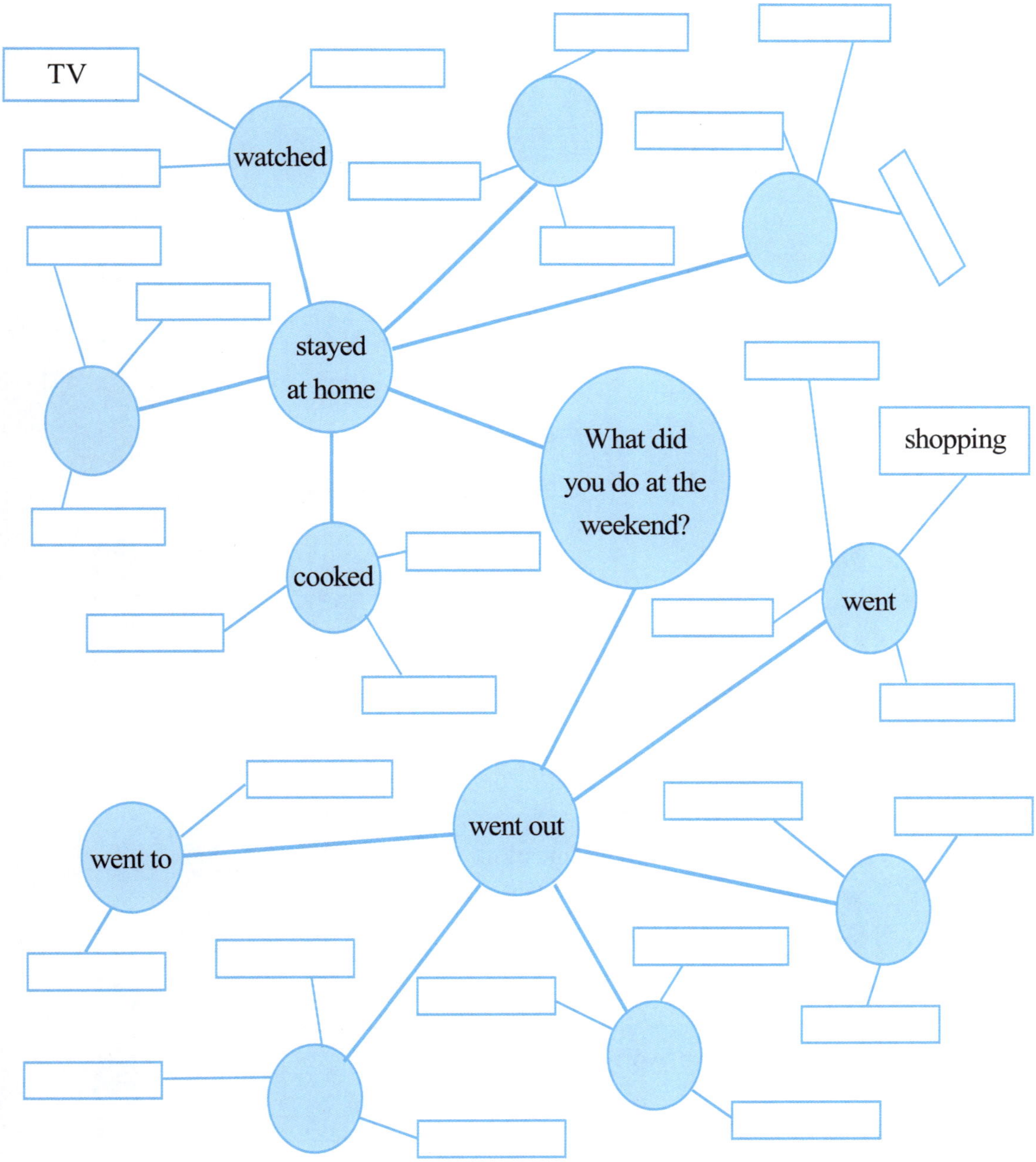

2. Discuss in groups again and try to give as many nouns or -ing participles as possible to each of the verbs in the squares in the above map, say, "went to" can be followed by "a park" "the zoo" "the library", etc.

3. Discuss with your partner and **work out** some sentences to be used when asking about and describing someone's weekend. You may also consult your teachers or the Internet.

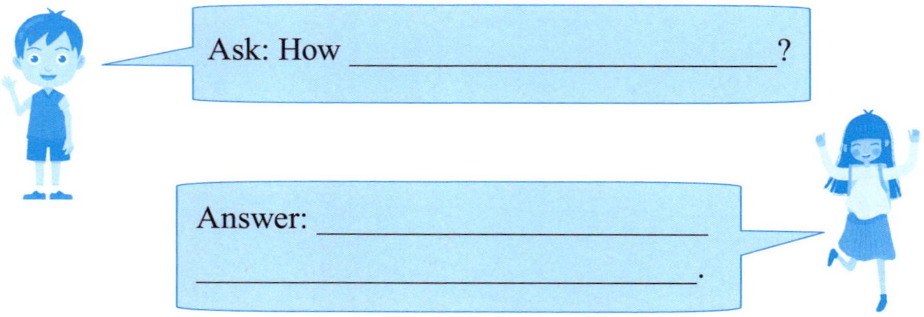

Or

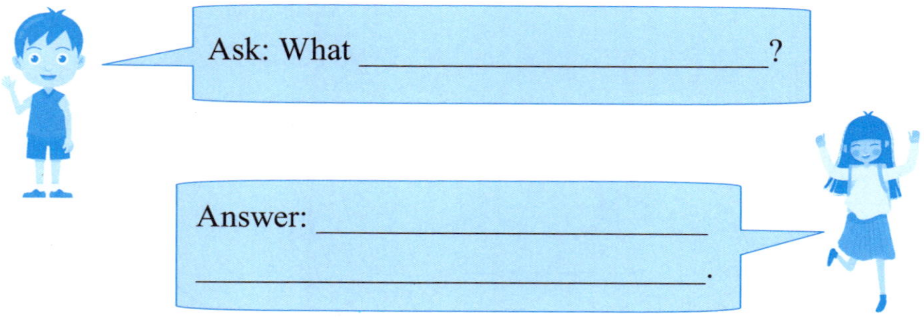

Then

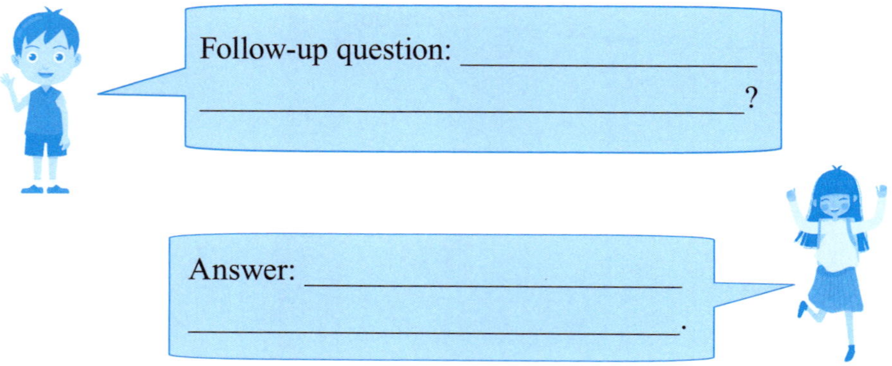

Or

Follow-up question: What else ____________

____?

Answer: ________________________________

____.

More (if you can)

Ask: Did ____?

Answer: ____.

Step 3 Speaking and Sharing

1. Work in pairs and take turns **asking** your partner about his or her last weekend by using the above sentences and questions.

2. Work in groups and **tell** them about your partner's weekend. You may begin your sharing with the following sentence patterns.

Language Kit

Last week, my friend… had a wonderful weekend. He/She…

3. Discuss in groups and **decide** who deserve the following medals. Each medal should be assigned to only one person. The last medal is for you to decide. You should take down the content of the medal first. When you name a candidate, you should tell others why you select him or her.

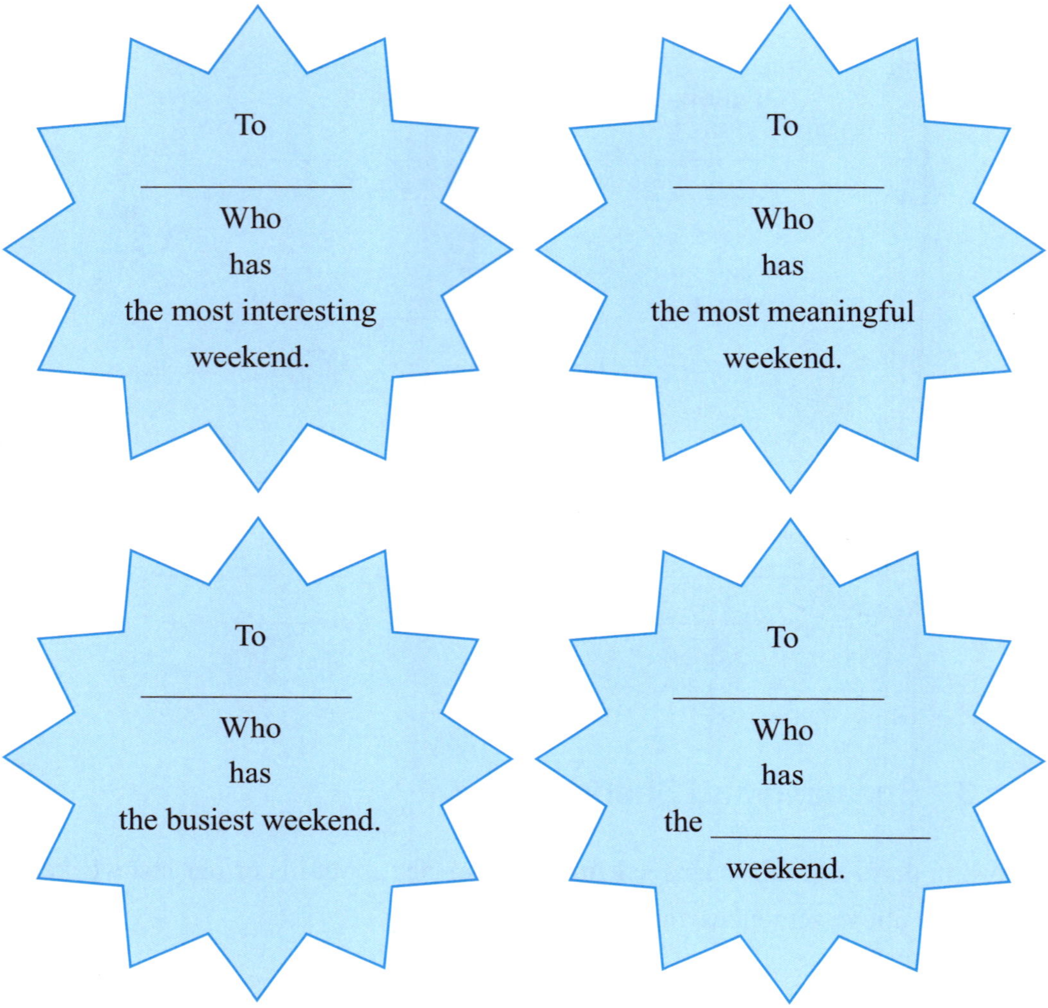

教学时长: 1.5 hrs

教学建议:

1. 听力理解环节。

（1）匹配题: 本题是听力练习前的语言准备活动，帮助学生回忆重点用语。

（2）学生听第一遍录音，完成两题。其中第2题，教师引导学生将活动与人物连线。

参考答案:

Grandpa: drank tea, watched TV

Mike: watched TV, cleaned the rooms, washed clothes

（3）学生听第二遍录音，完成两题。学生需要用所听到的内容填空。本题旨在引导学生注意询问的句式和回答用语。

参考答案：

What did; Did you do; was good; nice

2. 表达准备环节。

（1）学生在课堂上通过教师引导完成。

（2）活动1：本题旨在帮助学生回忆自己掌握的词汇并向同伴学习更多词汇，辅助学生学会这些动词的过去式形式，扩展教材内容，为表达与分享环节做准备。该思维图由"周末可以开展的活动"发散成两个方面："待在家"和"外出"。这两方面又各自联想出描述相关活动的动词，分别填写在圆圈里。注意：这一活动中学生只需填写思维图中的所有圆圈。教师要提醒学生只能填写动词的过去形式。

（3）活动2：学生给上述思维图中自己填写的动词（圆圈中）补充名词或动名词以完成对活动的描述。每个动词可搭配多个名词或动名词，如："went shopping/swimming/skating…, went to the gym/the zoo/the museum…"。

（4）活动3：学生思考询问周末活动的问句以及回答用语，均以一问一答为一组。其中，"Follow-up question"是在已经了解了对方的活动内容后需要进一步详细了解时所用的问句；"More"是让学生思考更多可用于询问活动情况或感受的用语。

参考答案：

Ask: How was your weekend?

Answer: It was good/bad/not bad/so so/boring/tiring/tedious...

Ask: What did you do last weekend?

Answer: I...

Follow-up question: What else did you do?

Answer: I...

Follow-up question: Did you...?

Answer: Yes, I did./No, I didn't.

3. 表达与分享环节。

（1）活动1：学生组内配对练习询问对方的周末情况，可参考表达准备环节中列举的活动。

（2）活动2：学生分小组，逐一向组员汇报自己对话伙伴的周末活动，参考“Language Kit”进行介绍。

（3）活动3：每个组员根据所听到的活动介绍来提名自己认为合适的奖章获得者，提名时需要简单说明理由（中文亦可）。小组共同商议确定奖章获得者，并将他们的名字写在对应的奖章上。教师需要讲解奖章的含义，分别是：“最有趣周末奖章”“最有意义周末奖章”和“最忙周末奖章”，可以允许同一人获得多枚奖章。最后一个奖章需要学生自行讨论设计，并将表特征的形容词最高级写进奖章中。教师可以给予提示，如“the most special weekend (最特别周末)” “the most productive weekend (最有成效的周末)” 等。

思维试纸：

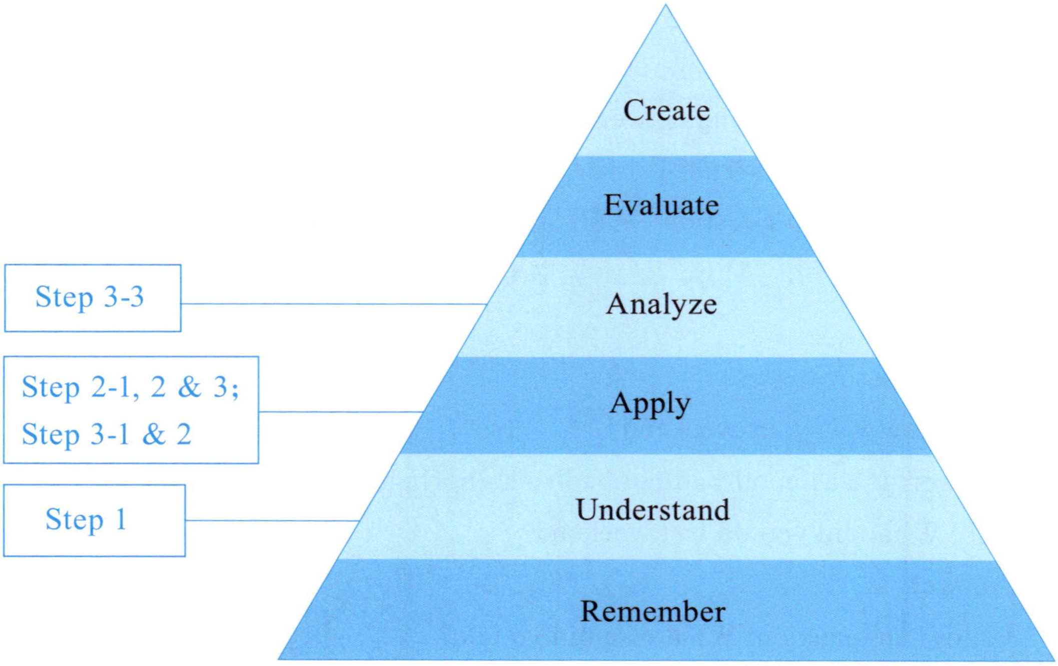

Part Two Reading and Writing

教学素材：Part B Read and Write

教学步骤：

Step 1 Preparation before Reading

1. Read the following sentences and tick the ones which you think can be used to **describe** something as a whole or make a summary in the end.

When we talk about or describe something happened in the past, we will describe it as a whole in the first sentence or make a summary in the end.

- □ (1) I fell off my bike and hurt my foot.
- □ (2) It was a busy weekend.
- □ (3) It is a bad day but also a good day!
- □ (4) There was no library in my school twenty years ago.
- □ (5) Once upon a time, there were three little pigs.
- □ (6) I had a very funny day on Saturday.

2. There is a short essay starting with the sentence "I had a very funny day on Saturday". What facts can show that the writer felt "funny"? **Decide** and tick them.

In conversation or writing, we will use some facts to support the general description or summary.

- □ (1) I wanted to ride with my friends but the bike was broken.
- □ (2) I went to picnic and met some little ducks. They enjoyed our lunch.
- □ (3) I got up early and had a wonderful breakfast.
- □ (4) I rode a bike for three people with my friends.
- □ (5) My friends and I dressed up and make a funny play at home.

3. Wu Yifan and his family stayed at the Holiday Hotel but it was not a happy time. Can you **imagine** what happened? Discuss in groups on what might make him and his family feel bad in the hotel. Take down your ideas below.

Why did they feel bad?

____

____

____

____

Step 2 Reading Comprehension

1. Read the letter in the textbook carefully and **understand** what happened to the family that day. Match the persons with the events.

A	B
Wu Yifan	wanted to read
Wu Yifan's mother	wanted to watch TV
Wu Yifan's father	got some hamburgers

2. Why did Wu Yifan's family feel bad? **Find** the facts and fill in the blanks.

Why did they feel bad?	
(1)	The room was big but ______________________.
(2)	Wu Yifan's mother wanted to read but ______________________.
(3)	Wu Yifan's father got some hamburgers but ______________________.
(4)	Wu Yifan wanted to watch TV but ______________________.
(5)	Wu Yifan wanted to sleep but ______________________.

Step 3 Writing and Sharing

1. What did you do last Sunday? How do you like it, good, bad, boring, interesting or meaningful? Try to complete the first sentence in the essay in Task 3 according to your own feelings.

2. Why did you have such a feeling towards last Sunday? List all the things happened or you did to **support** your feeling.

Why did you feel that way?	
(1)	
2	
3	
4	
...	...

3. **Rearrange** the above facts in order of time. Then add one or two more sentences to **describe** in detail and take all the sentences together down in the box below. You will get a complete essay.

A ___________ Sunday

Last Sunday I had a/an ______________________________ day. I
____
____
____
____
____
____
____

教学时长: 1 hr

教学建议:

1. 读前准备环节。

(1) 教师引导学生理解中心句的作用: 在口头叙述或书面叙述时的首句或末句, 通常会对所叙述的事件做一个总体评价。学生在所给句子中选择总结性评价。

参考答案: 2, 3, 6

(2) 教师引导学生理解如何为某一中心选择合适的事实依据, 即选择合适的事实来说明所做的总结评价。其中: ①我想和朋友一起骑自行车, 但是车坏了。这是不好的经历。②我们去野餐, 遇到了小鸭子, 它们吃掉了我们的午餐。结果出乎意料, 有趣。③我早上早起吃了一顿很棒的早餐。这是开始叙述一件事, 而不是有趣的经历。④我和朋友一起骑了三人自行车。重点在三人自行车, 不同寻常, 有趣。⑤我和朋友们在家开了一个有趣的化妆聚会。孩子们装扮起来肯定有很多有趣的事, 符合要求。

参考答案: 2, 4, 5

(3) 这一活动旨在通过让学生推测吴一凡一家在酒店有哪些不愉快的经历来帮助其做好阅读短文的心理、知识、语言准备。教师可安排学生分组讨论, 并把可能发生的情况用中文逐条写在题后的方框内。

2. 阅读理解环节。

(1) 连线题: 学生根据短文内容把人物和事件联系起来。

(2) 填空题: 学生根据短文内容填空, 梳理吴一凡一家不愉快的事实依据。教师可提醒学生注意单词 "but" 的用法和功能。

3. 写作与分享环节。

(1) 教师让学生回忆自己是如何度过上一个周日的并且对该经历用一个形容词进行总结性描述, 然后将该词填写在本部分第三题的短文首句空格处。教师需要帮助学生回忆有描述功能的形容词, 如 "good, bad, boring, interesting, meaningful, wonderful, productive, busy" 等。

(2) 教师引导学生根据自己的总体感受选择合适的事实作为依据并用一句话叙述该事件。对不适宜用一句话概述的事件, 教师引导学生写下该事件的首句, 为后续展开做好准备。事实依据不必规定数量, 应根据其书写的总体感受而确定。表格中所列序号为按需使用，不够可以自行添加，不足也无碍。

（3）学生将上一题表格中列举的事实根据时间顺序重新排列，然后视情况适当增加一两句话，并把所有句子都写在作文纸内，作文就写好了！学生可根据自己的能力决定作文长短，需做到条理清楚，事实依据合理。

思维试纸：

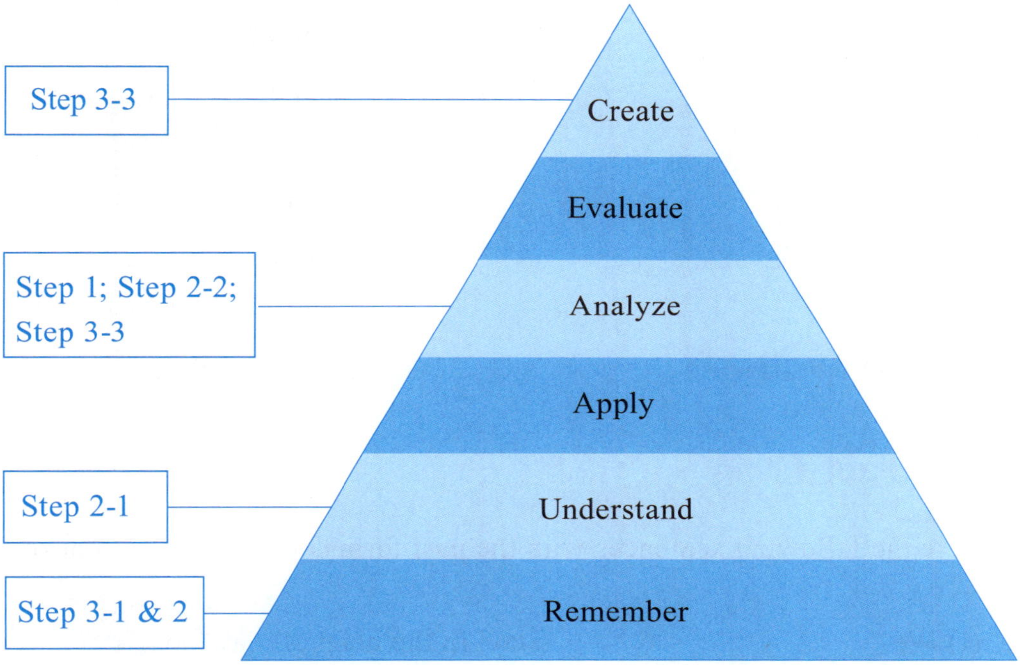

Part Three Vocabulary

教学素材：stayed, cleaned, watched, played, washed, talked, lived, wanted, planned, cooked, made, saw, slept, drank, did, had, read, went, was, got

教学步骤：

Step 1 Matching

Match the verbs in Column A with their corresponding past forms in Column B.

A	B
drink	made
do	saw
make	slept
is	got
read	drank
have	did
sleep	had
go	read
see	went
get	was

Step 2 Blank-filling

Complete the following sentences with the past forms of the verbs in brackets.

(1) We ____________________ (stay) in the hotel all day long.

(2) We ____________________ (clean) the classroom yesterday.

(3) He ____________________ (watch) TV with me that night.

(4) My dad and I ____________________ (play) volleyball this morning.

(5) At last, he ____________________ (wash) all his clothes.

(6) I ____________________ (talk) with him about our plan.

(7) We ____________________ (live) happily together for one year.

(8) She ____________________ (want) me to go to Spain with them.

(9) My friends ____________________ (plan) a party for me.

(10) I ____________________ (cook) some noodles for dinner.

教学时长: 20 mins

教学建议:

1. 词汇部分主要用于练习,旨在巩固词汇和语法知识。
2. 学生自行在课前或课后完成。课堂上,学生展示和分享作业,教师纠错。
3. "Step 1" 练习识别不规则动词的过去式形式。
4. "Step 2" 练习书写规则动词的过去式形式。

参考答案:

(1) stayed (2) cleaned (3) watched (4) played (5) washed
(6) talked (7) lived (8) wanted (9) planned (10) cooked

思维试纸:

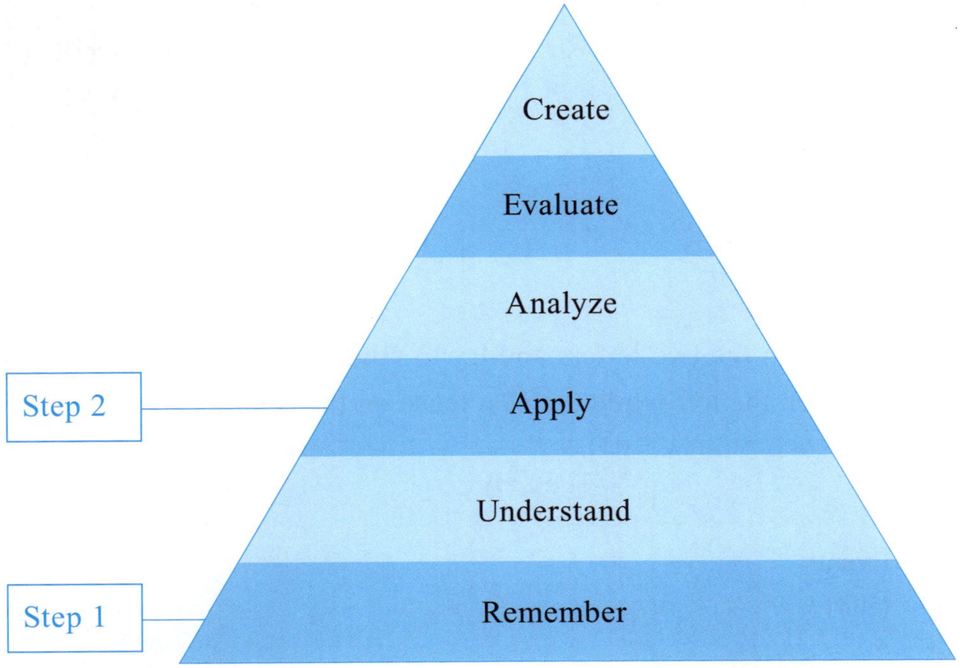

Part Four Grammar

教学素材: present tense of verbs and past tense of verbs

教学步骤:

Step 1　Self-checking

Read the two short letters below carefully and **circle** all the verbs in each of them.

Dear Binbin,

I like my new school. The school is beautiful and the teachers are wonderful.

Ms. Green teaches us English. She often sings English songs in class. She is my favorite teacher.

Mr. White is my art teacher. He is really good at drawing animals.

How do you like your teachers?

Yours,

Tim

Dear Amy,

Yesterday, we went on a school trip.

We went skating. I wore warm clothes. The ice was very cold.

At first, I fell over. But it didn't hurt a lot. Then I was able to skate. It was easy! And I didn't fall over again. It was really fun!

Love,

Lucy

Step 2　Rule-finding

Observe the verbs in the two letters and try to **find out** why the present tense is used in the letter on the left while the past tense on the right.

	The Left Letter	The Right Letter
Events (事件)		
Time (时间)		
…		

Step 3 Further Practicing

Fill in the blanks with the proper forms of the given verbs in brackets and complete the passage below.

On Sundays, I usually ___________ (ride) my bike to the park. And I usually ___________ (play) football in the park. But I ___________ (do not) ride my bike yesterday. And I ___________ (do not) play football in the park. It __________ (be) raining. I __________ (stay) at home and ___________ (clean) all the rooms. What a boring day!

教学时长: 30 mins

教学建议:

1. 语法部分主要用于练习，旨在巩固词汇和语法知识。本单元要求学生对比一般现在时和一般过去时，并在语境中正确运用时态。

学生自行在课前或课后完成，教师批改。

课堂上，教师带领学生总结存在的问题和解决办法。

2. 自我检测：该题要求学生圈出谓语动词，教师可做一两个示范。

3. 规则总结：教师引导学生观察两封信中时态使用的区别及原因：1）事件方面：左信没有提到具体的事件，而是对事实常态进行描述；右信叙述一件具体的事件。2）时间方面：左信描述的状态是当前很长一段时间的常态；右信描述的事件发生在过去。除以上两条原因或观测点以外，教师应鼓励学生总结其他原因。学生可以使用汉语讨论和填写。

4. 巩固练习：教师引导学生注意每句话叙述的事件和时间，以此来确定动词的时态。

参考答案：ride; play; didn't; didn't; was; stayed; cleaned

思维试纸:

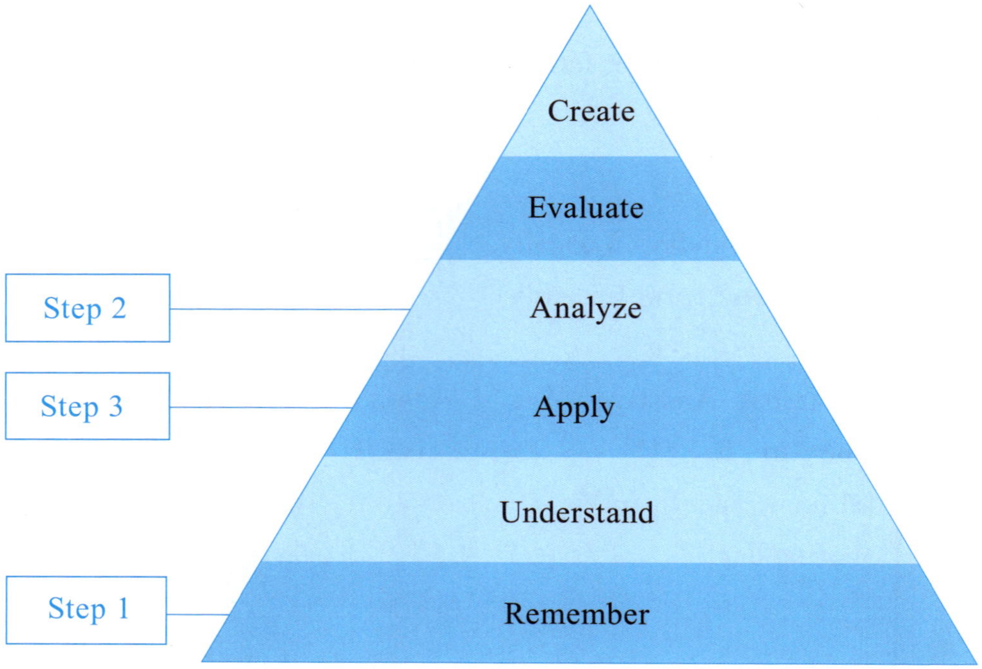
Create
Evaluate
Step 2
Analyze
Step 3
Apply
Understand
Step 1
Remember

Unit 3　Where Did You Go?

单元导览

单元话题: 节日安排

素材来源: PEP 6B Unit 3 Where Did You Go?

教学目标:

By the end of the lessons, students will be able to

语言目标:

1. **understand, write** and **use** the past forms of these verbs (eat, drink, run, go, take, put, can, buy, jump, lick, make, play, sit, ride, stay, want, laugh, see, hurt, fall) in linguistic context;

2. **describe** one's holiday by **using** past forms of the following: took pictures, ate delicious food, rode a bike, dressed up, played the part of a dog, bought gifts;

3. **use** general questions and special questions in past tense to **ask for** one's holiday;

4. **understand** the conversations in the textbook and **ask about** one's holiday with the sentence patterns: "How did you get there?" "Where did you go over the summer holiday?" "What did you do there?" "How was…?";

5. **comprehend** the meaning of the passage, **analyze** the main content and structure, and **apply** the knowledge and language in the essay to **rewriting** it based on their own understanding.

非语言目标:

1. learn to be optimistic when facing problems in life;

2. learn the positive qualities of excellent students;

3. **classify** words and expressions according to their features, functions and contents;

4. strengthen their higher order thinking skills: **analyzing, evaluating** and **creating**;

5. **sort out** answers and **predict** results with logic **reasoning**.

融思设计

Part One　Listening and Speaking

教学素材: Part B　Let's Talk

教学步骤:

Step 1　Listening Comprehension

Listen to the conversation and **complete** the following table. Only one word is allowed in each blank.

Amy's Winter Holiday			
Destination (目的地)	Transportation (交通工具)	Activities	Feelings
________	By ________	She ________ lots of ________ and ________.	It was ________; The beach was ________.

Step 2　Preparation before Speaking

1. The following questions can be used to ask about one's holidays. **Put** them into the table below according to the context.

A. How did you get there?
B. Did you like it?
C. Where did you go over the summer holiday?
D. How was your winter holiday?
E. What did you do there?
F. How did you spend your holiday?
G. Did you go by train?

Contents	The Number of the Questions
Destination	
Transportation	
Activities	
Feelings	

2. Besides the these questions, are there any other questions can be used to ask about someone's holiday? If yes, **take** them **down** in the above table.

Step 3 Speaking and Sharing

1. Work in groups and **ask** each group member about his or her winter holiday by **using** the questions in Step 2.

2. Discuss in groups and **find** appropriate person(s) to fill in the following report sheet.

Questions	Answers
Whose trip is the farthest?	
Who thought that his/her holiday was good?	
Who went on holiday by train?	
Whose holiday is the most interesting?	

3. Ambassador visit: Each group member should go to one of the rest groups and **report** the result of your survey to them and why your group choose that person.

教学时长: 1.5 hrs

教学建议:

1. 听力理解环节。

听音填空。教师可视学生情况决定播放录音的次数。学生用听到的内容填表。每个空只能填写一个单词。

参考答案:

Amy's Winter Holiday			
Destination (目的地)	Transportation (交通工具)	Activities	Feelings
Sanya	By plane	She took lots of pictures and went swimming.	It was warm; The beach was beautiful.

2. 表达准备环节。

(1) 课堂上, 教师引导学生完成各项活动。

(2) 活动1: 学生仔细阅读所有问题, 根据问题的内容将它们分别分配到不同的类别去。其中 "D. How was your winter holiday?" 询问的内容比较广, 本书界定其为询问感受。

参考答案:

Contents	The Number of the Questions
Destination	C
Transportation	A, G
Activities	E, F
Feelings	B, D

(3) 活动2: 教师可以启发学生从“who”和“details (细节)”来思考适合的问句, 如: “Who went with you?” “How was…” “Did you…”。

3. 表达与分享环节。

(1) 活动1: 学生分组活动, 每个组员都要与其他所有组员分别交谈, 利用“Step 2”里面提到的问题询问他(她)寒假的活动。

(2) 活动2: 小组分析每个组员的假期活动, 选择适当的人选填进调查表中。调查表中的第2、3问可以选择多人, 第1、4问只能选择一人。

(3) 活动3: 这是一个“大使出访”游戏, 每个组员去另一个组介绍本组的调查结果, 并介绍原因。每个组员要去往不同的小组。

思维试纸:

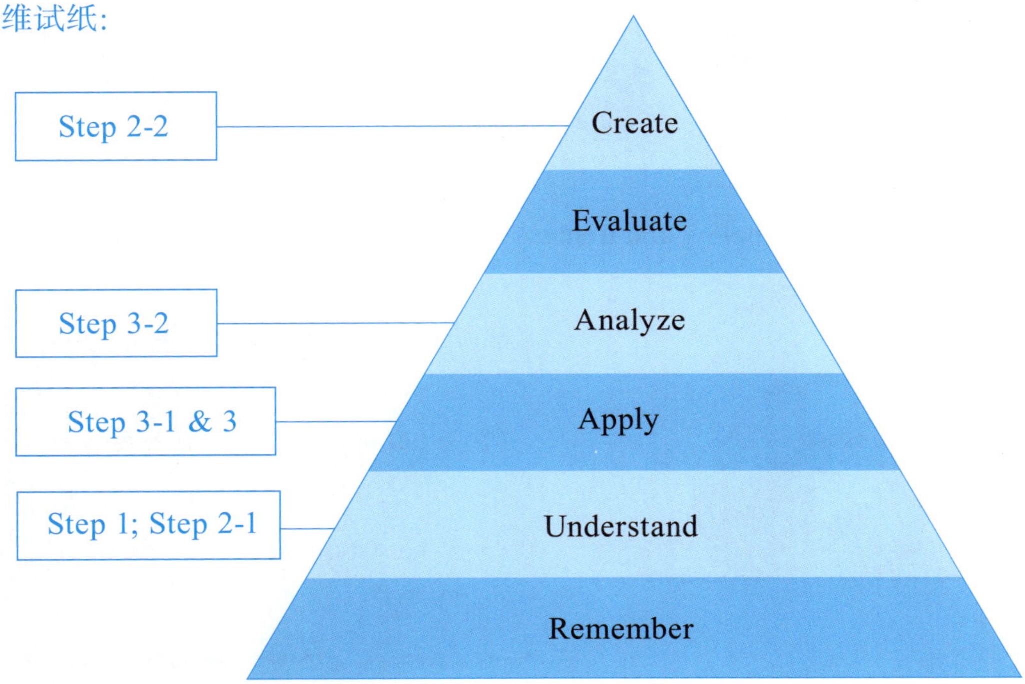

Part Two Reading and Writing

教学素材: Part B Read and Write

教学步骤:

Step 1 Preparation before Reading

1. What happened in these pictures? **Match** the pictures with the phrases below.

took pictures

rode a bike

ate delicious food

bought gifts

dressed up

played the part of a dog

2. Look at the picture below and **discuss** the following questions in pairs.

(1) What can you see in the picture?

(2) What happened to the family?

(3) What would Wu Yifan do then?

Step 2 Reading Comprehension

1. Read the passage and **summarize** what the family did in the morning and in the afternoon. Then **complete** the sentences in the **circles** in the diagram below. Only one word is allowed in each blank.

A ____________ but ____________ Day

MORNING

They ______ ______ ______.

Activities
- ☺☹ They ______ ______.
- ☺☹ They ______ ______.
- ☺☹ They ______ ______ ______.

Feeling
- That ______ ______.

AFTERNOON

They ______ in the hotel.

Problem
- ☺☹ Mother didn't ____________ ____________. They had to ____________ in the hotel.

Solution
- ☺☹ They ______ ______ and made a ______ ______. Max ______ on Robin and ______ him.

Feeling
- They all ____________.

2. Read the passage again. **Find** the details of their day and complete the sentences in the squares in the diagram. Only one word is allowed in each blank.

Step 3 Preparation before Writing

Why did Wu Yifan say "it was a bad but good day"? What do you think is good and what is bad on that day? Tick the smiling face ☺ above the thing(s) you think is (are) good in the diagram and the crying face ☹ above the thing(s) you think is (are) bad.

Step 4　Writing and Sharing

Rearrange your ideas to produce a new passage about "A Day of Wu Yifan and His Family" and fill in the following blanks.

A Day of Wu Yifan and His Family

Wu Yifan and his family had a ______________________ day. It was a bad day because ____.

But it was still a good day. In the morning, ____.

In the afternoon, they ____.

教学时长: 1 hr

教学建议:

1. 读前准备环节。

（1）活动1: 学生将图片与短语连线。教师可以安排学生课前完成。

（2）活动2（口头表达练习）: 学生先在小组内口头描述和讨论。然后, 每组派代表在全班描述。教师引导学生按照顺序逐题叙述。第一题, 每位同学用 "I can see..." 来详细讲述在图片上看到的内容; 第二题, 小组讨论图片中可能发生了什么情况; 第三题, 小组讨论吴一凡会怎么解决图片中的问题或者接下来他会怎么做。

2. 阅读理解环节。

（1）教师要求学生按照每题的指示（每一步骤务必填写指定圆圈内的空格）完成练习并提示学生需要提炼原文进行填空。

（2）活动1: 学生读一遍短文, 填写图表中圆圈内的空格。每个空格只填一词。

（3）活动2：学生再读一遍短文，填写图表中方框内的空格。每个空格只填一词。

参考答案：

A __Bad__ but __Good__ Day

MORNING

They __rode__ __a__ __bike__ .

Activities
- They __took__ __pictures__ .
- They __bough__ __gifts__ .
- They __ate__ __delicious__ __food__ .

Feeling
- That __was__ __funny__ .

AFTERNOON

They __stayed__ in the hotel.

Problem
- Mother didn't __feel__ __well__ . They had to __stay__ in the hotel.

Solution
- They __dressed__ __up__ and made a __funny__ __play__ . Max __jumped__ on Robin and __licked__ him.

Feeling
- They all __laughed__ .

3. 写前准备环节。

学生单独思考为什么吴一凡认为这是不愉快但是美好的一天。然后，学生在第二环节的图表中用笑脸图案标注所有美好的事件，用哭脸图案标注不愉快的事件。

4. 写作与分享环节。

这是一个短文改写练习。教师引导学生将自己认为原文中美好的事物和不愉快的事物分别梳理、总结，适当增减语言，填写进短文框架里。

思维试纸:

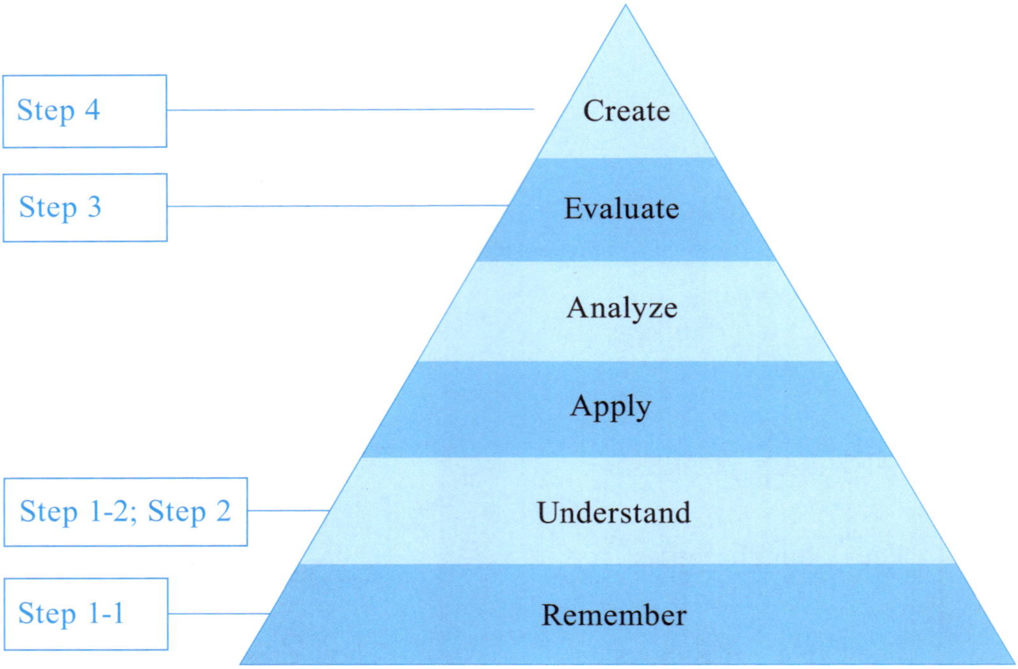

Part Three　Vocabulary

教学素材: ate, drank, ran, went, took, put, could, bought, jumped, licked, made, played, sat, rode, stayed, wanted, laughed, saw, hurt, fell

教学步骤:

Step 1　Blank-filling

Write the past forms of the verbs below.

(1) eat → ________　　(2) drink → ________

(3) run → ________　　(4) go → ________

(5) take → ________　　(6) can → ________

(7) buy → ________　　(8) lick → ________

(9) make → ________　　(10) play → ________

(11) sit	→ ____________	(12) ride	→ ____________
(13) stay	→ ____________	(14) want	→ ____________
(15) fall	→ ____________	(16) jump	→ ____________
(17) put	→ ____________	(18) laugh	→ ____________
(19) see	→ ____________	(20) hurt	→ ____________

Step 2 Analyzing and Selecting

Group the above verbs into different types according to the features in the following clouds. Then, set your own standard to fill in the last cloud and **select** proper verbs.

规则动词:

不规则动词:

会用到嘴的动作:

____________________:

教学时长：20 mins

教学建议：

1. 词汇部分主要用于练习，旨在巩固词汇知识。

2. 学生自行在课前或课后完成。课堂上，学生展示和分享作业，教师纠错。

3. “Step 1”练习转换动词过去式形式。

参考答案：

(1) ate	(2) drank	(3) ran	(4) went	(5) took
(6) could	(7) bought	(8) licked	(9) made	(10) played
(11) sat	(12) rode	(13) stayed	(14) wanted	(15) fell
(16) jumped	(17) put	(18) laughed	(19) saw	(20) hurt

4. “Step 2”要求学生根据分类特征把“Step 1”所列动词中符合条件的放到该类中去。注意：教师提醒学生填写动词的过去形式。教师需要鼓励学生开动脑筋确定更多标准或特征来对这些动词进行分类，并把分类标准和选择的动词写在最后一个图形里。

思维试纸：

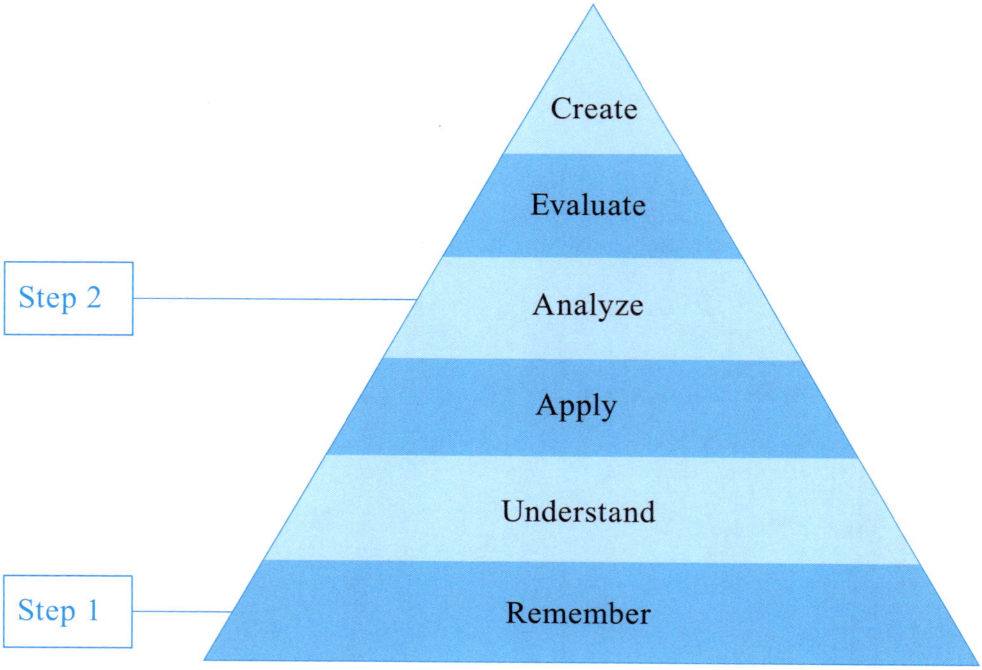

Part Four Grammar

教学素材: 1. The general questions in past tense;

2. The special questions in past tense.

教学步骤:

Step 1 Self-checking

Use the word in brackets to ask a question on the underlined part in each sentence.

(1) I <u>hurt</u> my foot. (did)

____

(2) I went to <u>Qingdao</u> over the summer holiday. (where)

____

(3) I <u>watched a movie</u> last Sunday. (what)

____

(4) We all felt <u>happy</u> in that English class. (how)

____

(5) <u>Mr. Li</u> was my English teacher in Grade Three. (who)

____

Step 2 Rule-finding

1. **Observe** the questions below carefully and **find** the word which is in each question. Write the word down on the line.

____

- Did you go to Turpan?
- Where did you go last Saturday?
- What did they do yesterday?
- Who did you buy a gift for?
- How did you feel?

2. Discuss in groups and **summarize** the rules of making a question when the verb of the sentence is a notional verb. Write down your ideas below.

当谓语动词是实义动词时：

实义动词即行为动词，表示动作的动词。它是意思完整、能独立用作谓语的动词，包括及物动词和不及物动词。

3. **Observe** the questions below carefully and **circle** verb "be" in all of them.

- Was it beautiful?
- How was the beach?
- Where were you at that time?
- Were you happy?

4. Discuss in groups and **summarize** the rules of making a question when the verb of the sentence is the verb "be". Write down your ideas below.

当谓语动词是be动词时：

Step 3 Further Practicing

Who were my teacher's favorite students?

1. There is a picture of your teacher's former students. Two of them were your teacher's favorite ones. Do you want to know who they were? You can **find out** by asking your teacher a lot of questions. But you can only ask general questions in past tense, such as "Was it a boy?" "Did he wear glasses?" Your teacher will only answer with "Yes" or "No".

2. Congratulations on finding out your teacher's favorite students. Do you want to know why your teacher liked them? You can also get the reasons by asking questions. This time, you can **ask** both general questions like the above ones and the wh-questions in past tense. But you cannot ask "why". Your teacher will answer your questions briefly.

教学时长: 40 mins

教学建议:

1. 语法部分主要用于练习，旨在巩固语法知识。本单元要求学生掌握运动一般过去时的一般疑问句和特殊疑问句。

2. Step 1 and Step 2: 学生自行在课前或课后完成，教师批改。课堂上，教师带领学生总结存在的问题和解决办法。

3. Step 3: 学生课堂上完成。教师自行准备一张以往学生的合影（包括男女生），确定两名自己最喜欢的学生，并预设好他们获得教师青睐的原因，这些原因要足以成为学生学习的榜样。活动开始时，教师将该照片出示给全班学生（使用PPT或实物投影仪），让学生观察并提问。

（1）学生通过用一般疑问句（一般过去时）提问来找出老师最喜欢的两名学生。每位同学一次只能问一个问题。教师只能回答"Yes" 或 "No"，不提供细节信息。

（2）当学生找出这两名学生以后，学生将通过一般疑问句或特殊疑问句（一般过去时）来找出教师青睐这两名学生的理由，但不能问“why”。教师要根据事先预设好的理由简要回答学生的提问，回答不必详细，以此促使学生多提问题。

思维试纸：

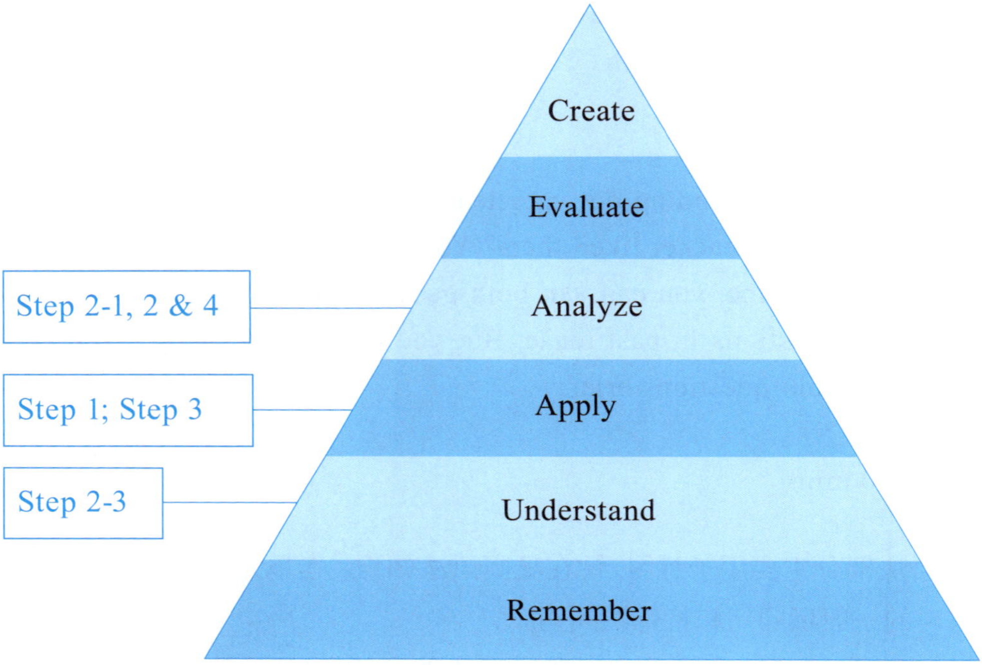

Unit 4 Then and Now

单元导览

单元话题：日常活动

素材来源：PEP 6B Unit 4 Then and Now

教学目标：

By the end of the lessons, students will be able to

语言目标：

1. **understand**, **write** and **use** the past forms of these verbs (give, feel, trip, wake, look, change) in linguistic context;

2. **use** the negative form of past tense to express what were or happened in the past;

3. **understand** the conversations in the textbook and talk about their own changes from Grade One with the sentence pattern: ...but now, ...;

4. **comprehend** the meaning of the passage, **analyze** the main content and structure, and **apply** the knowledge and language in the essay to writing an essay about their own dream or about a given story;

5. **tell** the differences between present tense and past tense and use both tenses correctly to **describe** what happened and what is happening.

非语言目标：

1. learn to be optimistic and positive towards one's own growth;

2. **analyze** the basic elements of an event and its time sequence with **information-seeking, interpreting** and **judging** skills.

3. develop their divergent thinking;

4. strengthen their higher order thinking skills: **analyzing**, **evaluating** and **creating**.

5. find mistakes and correct them with **decision-making** and **problem-solving** skills.

融思设计

Part One　Listening and Speaking

教学素材: Part B　Let's Talk

教学步骤:

Step 1　Listening Comprehension

Listen and **fill in** the blanks. Only one word is allowed in each blank.

Mike

Past	Now
He was wearing a ______ T-shirt.	He doesn't ______ pink.
He was ______.	He is ______ in class.

John

Past	Now
He was ______.	
He couldn't ______ his ______ well.	He ______ ______ every day.

Step 2 Preparation before Speaking

1. Did you also change a lot from Grade One till now? How can you tell your changes to others? **Brainstorm** in groups on the words or phrases you can use and write them down in the mind map below. You may add more aspects.

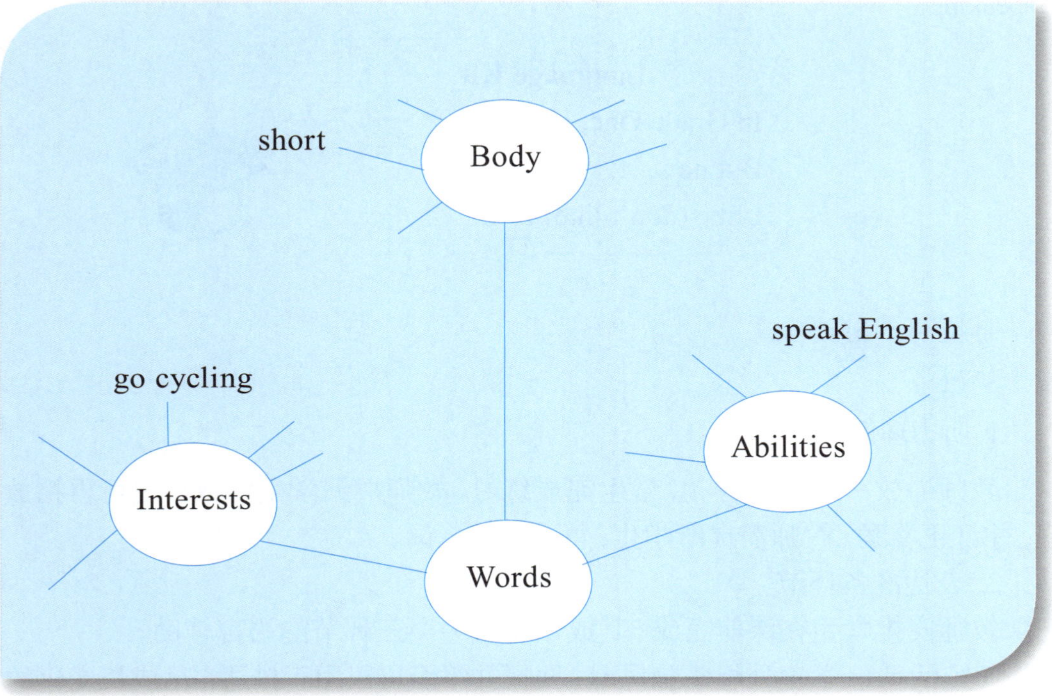

2. How do you feel about your own changes? There are some sentences to say that you like these changes. But what can you say if you don't like them? **Change** these sentences into negative forms and write in the right column.

Positive Form	Negative Form
I like to get older.	
I like these changes.	
I am happy with these changes.	
It's good to get older.	

Step 3 Speaking and Sharing

1. **Summarize** your own changes from Grade One till now. How do you feel about them?

2. Tell your partner all your changes. You may follow the framework below when speaking.

Language Kit

In Grade One, I…

But now, …

I like (don't like)/to…

教学时长: 1.5 hrs

教学建议:

1. 听力理解环节。

教师播放一遍对话音频，学生完成练习。教师根据学生完成情况可再播放一遍，并订正答案。教师需提醒学生，每空只填一词。

2. 表达准备环节。

教师安排学生在课前完成。其成果将成为第三环节的语言辅助。

（1）活动1：学生分组头脑风暴，回忆并组织可以用于描述自己成长变化的词汇和短语。学生应根据所给三个方向发散联想并完成思维图，也可以增加其他方面信息。

（2）活动2旨在帮助学生准备总结成长感受的语言。学生应将所给语句转换成否定句并填写进表格中。

参考答案：

I don't like to get older. I don't like these changes.

I am not happy with these changes. It's not good to get older.

3. 表达与分享环节。

（1）学生课前完成思考和语言准备。

（2）两个学生轮流进行口头叙述练习，叙述时需要按照所给框架进行，并可参考第二环节准备的用语。注意，不是对话练习。

（3）扩展活动（教师视情况选用）：学生自愿向全班展示。

思维试纸:

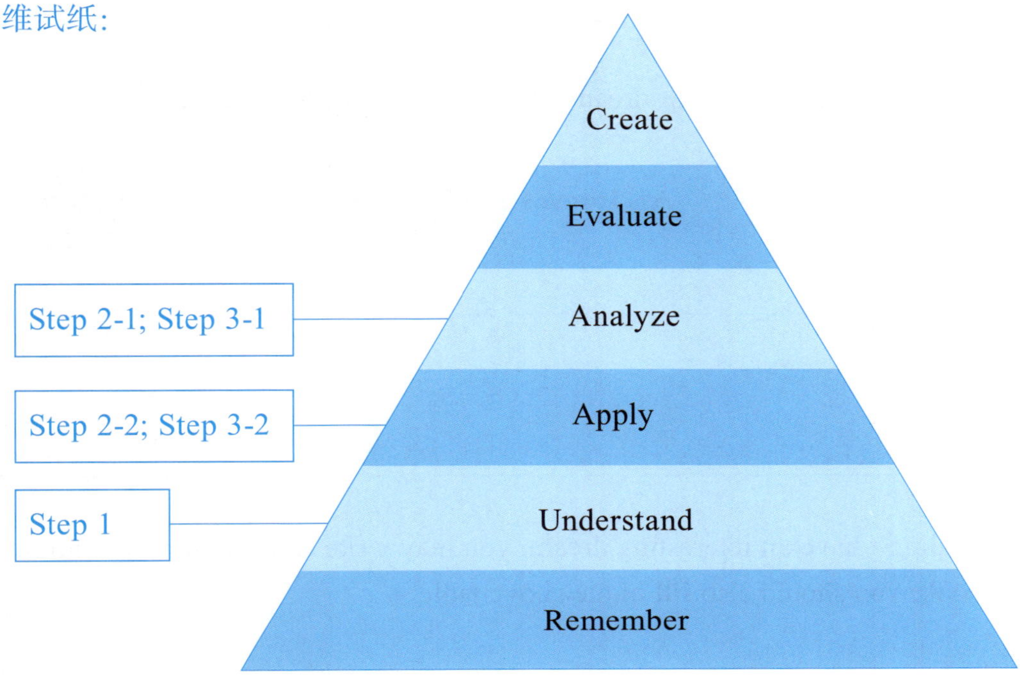

Part Two Reading and Writing

教学素材: Part B Read and Write

教学步骤:

Step 1 Reading Comprehension

Read and **fill in** the table below.

A Dream of Wu Yifan	
Who	Wu Yifan, his ________, ________, ________
What	Wu Yifan ________ ________ ________ with his father and Max but he couldn't ________ ________.
Ending	Robin __________ him some water. Wu Yifan __________ it and then he __________ very fast. He could ________ but he ________ and ____________.

Step 2　Preparation before Writing

1. Did you have an interesting dream? **Write** some words or sentences about your dream in the table below.

An Interesting Dream	
Who	
What	
Ending	

2. If you didn't have an interesting dream, you may write about Zoom's dream in the textbook. You should also **fill in** the above table.

Step 3　Writing and Sharing

1. Put all the above words and sentences together and **make** an essay. Cross out the title in the bracket and tick "I" and "my" in the sentences below.

An Interesting Dream (A Dream of Zoom)

Last ________ (I/Zoom) had a dream. In (my/his) dream, ________
____
____
____
____
____
____

What a dream!

2. If you will write about Zoom's dream, put all the above words and sentences together and make an essay under the title of "A Dream of Zoom". Tick the title in brackets and tick "Zoom" and "his" in the above sentences.

教学时长: 1 hr

教学建议:

1. 阅读理解环节。

教师引导学生根据表格结构梳理故事情节和内容，并填写空格，一空一词。

参考答案：

father; Robin; Max; had a race; run fast; gave; drank; ran; win; tripped; fell

2. 写前准备环节。

(1) 活动1：学生用几句话或人名将自己的梦所涉及的人、事件和结果记录在表格中。

(2) 活动2：这是针对不便描述自己梦境的备选方案。学生可以根据教材中关于"Zoom"的梦境的内容，完成活动1。

3. 写作与分享环节。

(1) 活动1：学生课后完成。适当扩展"Step 2"表格中的信息和语句，并按照时间顺序描述梦境。

(2) 活动2：这是针对不便描述自己梦境的备选方案。学生利用"Step 2"表格中语句转述"Zoom"的梦境，短文题目改为"A Dream of Zoom"。

思维试纸:

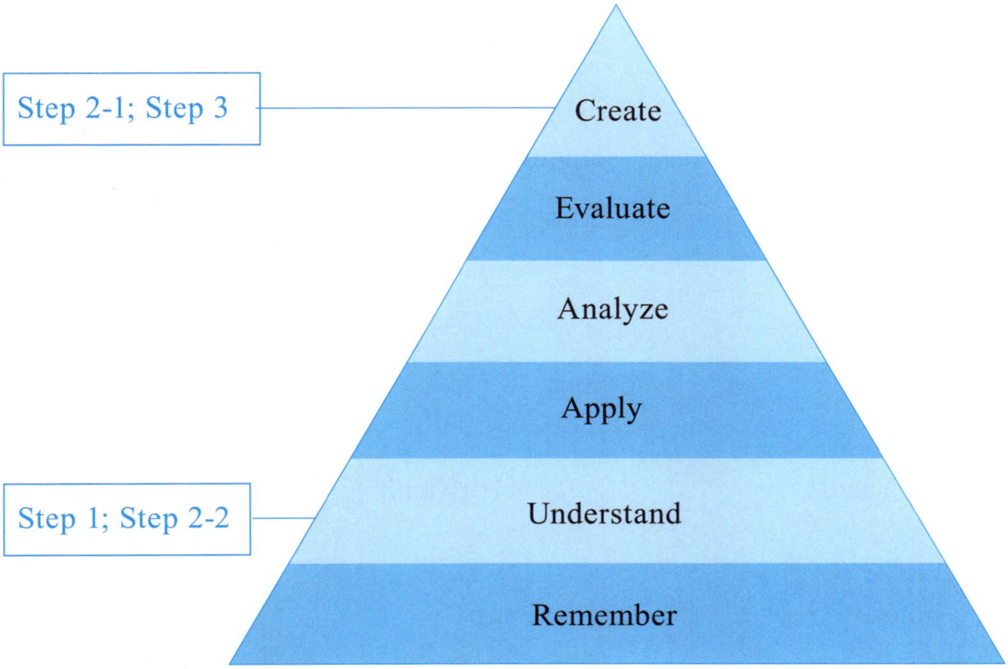

Part Three Vocabulary

教学素材: gave, felt, tripped, woke, looked, changed, grass, cycling, star, ice, nothing, active, easy, badminton, different, race, trip, dream, cheetah

教学步骤:

Step 1 Word-seeking

Circle letters to make words. The example is given below.

b	a	d	m	i	n	t	o	n	d
w	t	r	i	p	a	r	t	z	i
c	h	e	e	t	a	h	a	l	f
y	e	a	s	y	c	a	m	p	f
c	z	m	e	a	t	r	a	c	e
l	n	o	t	h	i	n	g	o	r
i	c	e	t	i	v	e	h	u	e
n	j	w	o	k	e	p	t	l	n
g	r	a	s	s	t	a	r	d	t

Step 2 Matching

Link two words together which are opposite in meaning to each other to make a pair. The example is given below.

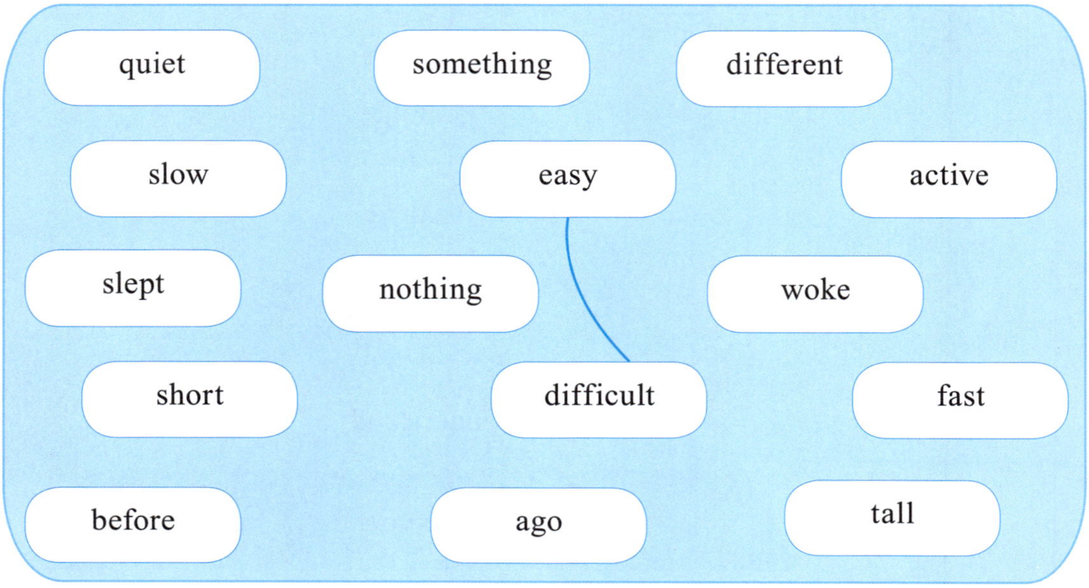

教学时长: 20 mins

教学建议:

1. 词汇部分主要用于练习，旨在巩固词汇和语法知识。
2. 学生自行在课前或课后完成，教师批改。
3. 课堂上，教师带领学生总结存在的问题和解决办法。

参考答案:

Step 1（下图只是一部分单词。鼓励学生寻找尽可能多的单词）:

b	a	d	m	i	n	t	o	n	d
w	t	r	i	p	a	r	t	z	i
c	h	e	e	t	a	h	a	l	f
y	e	a	s	y	c	a	m	p	f
c	z	m	e	a	t	r	a	c	e
l	n	o	t	h	i	n	g	o	r
i	c	e	t	i	v	e	h	u	e
n	j	w	o	k	e	p	t	l	n
g	r	a	s	s	t	a	r	d	t

Step 2:

quiet—active; slept—woke; nothing—something; ago—before; different—same; easy—difficult; short—tall; fast—slow

思维试纸:

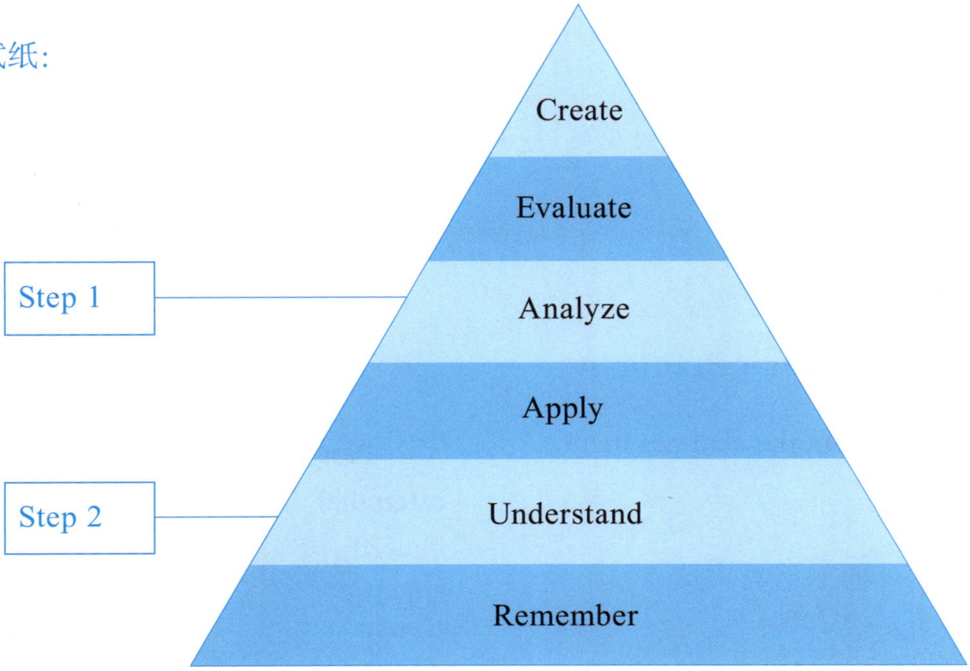

Part Four　Grammar

教学素材: 1. The negative form of past tense;

2. Differences between present tense and past tense.

教学步骤:

Step 1　Self-checking

There is a mistake in each sentence below. **Underline** the mistake and then **write down** the correct sentence.

(1) There are many clean rivers in the past.

____

(2) Wu Yifan runs like a cheetah in the race.

____

(3) What you dreamed about?

____

(4) Did you can see stars here at night ten years ago?

____

(5) There was a gym in our school now.

____

(6) People went not by bus in the Tang Dynasty.

____

Step 2　Further Practicing

1. **Write** about the changes below.

Language Kit

caterpillar 毛毛虫

butterfly 蝴蝶

crawl 爬行

(1) It ______________________.

Now, it ______________________.

(2) The light ______________________.

Now, ______________________.

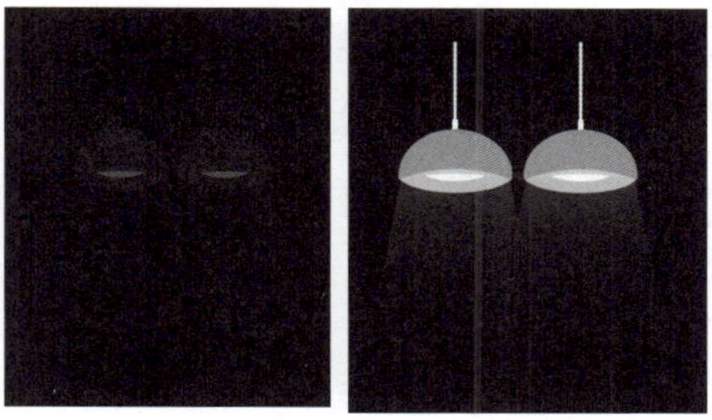

(3) There ______________________.

But now, ______________________.

(4) Children ______________________.

Now, ______________________.

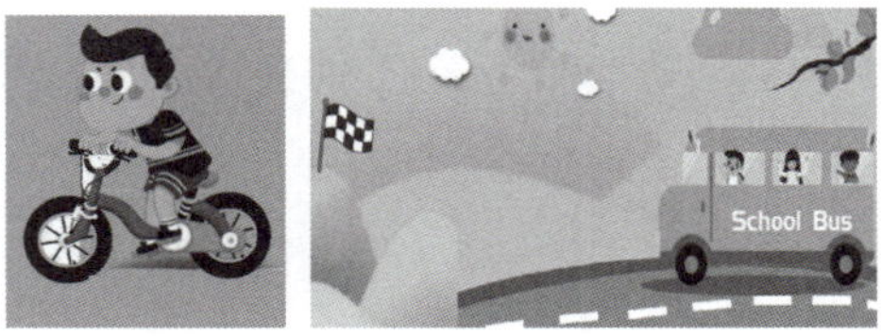

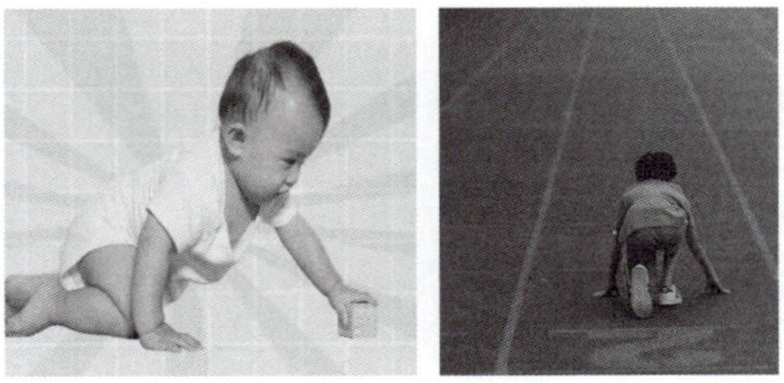

(5) When I was one year old, I ____________

______________________.

Now, I ______________________.

2. **Write** more pairs of sentences about "Then and Now". Share with your group members.

Then and Now

教学时长: 20 mins

教学建议:

1. 语法部分主要用于练习，旨在巩固语法知识。
2. 学生自行在课前或课后完成，教师批改。
3. 课堂上，教师带领学生总结存在的问题和解决办法。

参考答案:

活动1:

(1) There are many clean rivers in the past.

There were many clean rivers in the past.

(2) Wu Yifan runs like a cheetah in the race.

Wu Yifan ran like a cheetah in the race.

(3) What you dreamed about?

What did you dream about?

(4) Did you can see stars here at night five years ago?

Could you see stars here at night five years ago?

(5) There <u>was</u> a gym in our school now.

There is a gym in our school now.

(6) People <u>went not</u> by bus in the Tang Dynasty.

People did not go by bus in the Tang Dynasty.

活动2:

(1) It was a caterpillar. Now, it is a butterfly.

(2) The light was off. Now, it is on.

(3) There was a forest. But now, there is a building.

(4) Children went to school by bike. Now, they go to school by bus.

(5) When I was one year old, I could only crawl. Now, I can run.

思维试纸:

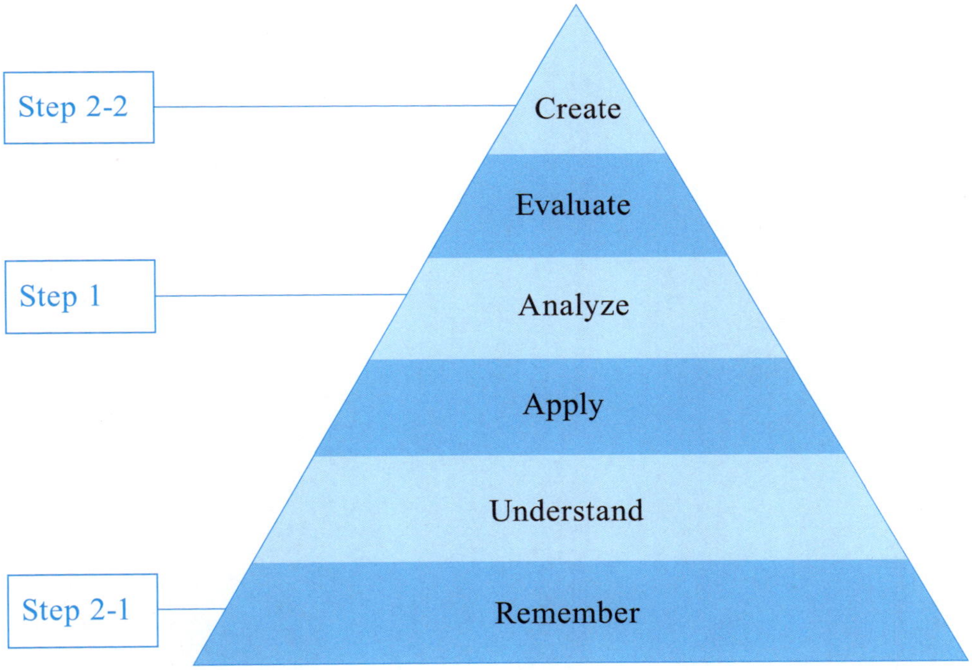